Pi

WINNING FROM FAILING

"Business has never been better. Thank you, Josh, for being our coach and helping us develop a learning culture!"

—**CHRISTOPHER T. EDWARDS,** President, ACW Management Corporation

"Process is the guiding force for success in all things. Disciplined organizations and world-class athletes drive to and through their goals by using processes specifically created to achieve success. In this book, Josh Seibert clearly challenges you, the leader, to create the processes needed to reach world-class levels of success."

—**STEVE SCOTT,** President, Tri-State Steel

"Doing business today is more and more about how the cultures of organizations align and how mutual stakeholders can identify win-win solutions. This requires new tools and fresh approaches. In his new book, Josh Seibert shows how to build sales and business development teams around a powerful learning-oriented culture."

—**ROYSTER TUCKER III,** CEO, North State Communications

"Josh has a great way of inspiring us to understand the culture we work in and continue on the path of learning with our people. This starts by understanding the four roles for a manager, but along the way we see the engagement and commitment it takes from everyone in an organization. *Winning from Failing* offers specific examples that allow readers to grasp the power of methodology, reinforcement, and benchmarking."

—**MARK J. TUCKER,** Senior Vice President of Sales, Blue Rhino

"If you are looking to help drive change and development within yourself or your organization, this book is a must-read."

—**CHRIS TREVEY,** President, Carlton Scale

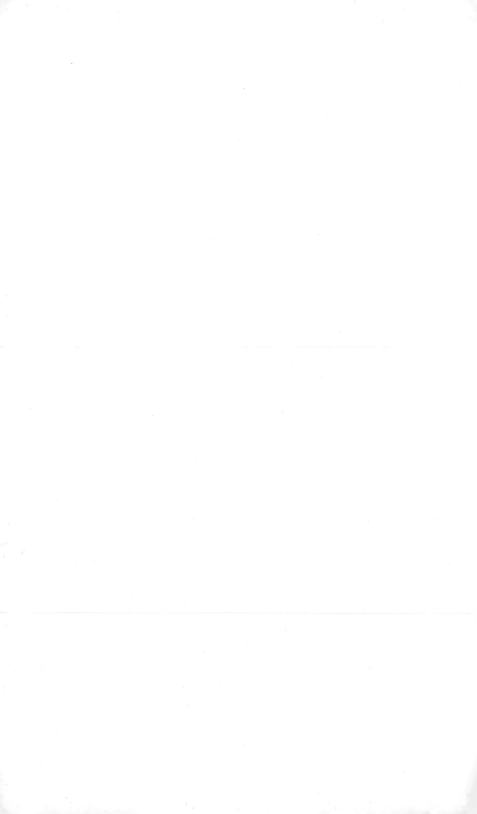

WINNING

— FROM —

FAILING

WINNING ⊢ FROM ⊣ FAILING

Build and Lead a Corporate Learning Culture for High Performance

JOSH SEIBERT

Sandler Training®

Paperback ISBN: 978-0-692-83858-7

E-book ISBN: 978-0-692-83859-4

To Almighty God, who gives the blessing of life itself.

To my bride since 1977, Ann Seibert, for unfailing love and support.

To our daughters Colleen Kelly, Carey Ann, and Angela Joy, all of whom I feel more proud of with every passing day.

To my late father and mother, Stanley and Joy Seibert. They instilled in me the value of honor and provided everlasting inspiration.

To my country, the United States of America, for providing me with the freedom to pursue my dreams and for allowing me the honor and the privilege of having served in the U.S. Navy's submarine force.

I'd like to express my deep gratitude for:

- The leadership of David Mattson, his courage in perpetually driving in the fast lane, and all of my friends at Sandler Corporate who help him change the tires along the way.
- The professionalism, dedication, and undying energy of my colleagues in the incredible network of Sandler trainers.
- The patience and guidance, throughout this journey, of Yusuf Toropov. Yusuf, I could not have done this without you.
- The masterful illustration, layout, and editing work of Jerry Dorris and Laura Matthews.
- The loyalty and commitment of all the team members at the Sandler franchise, Training & Development Solutions, Inc., the land of misfit toys.

CONTENTS

FOREWORD

David Sandler, the founder of our company, famously said, "You have to learn to fail, to win." It sounds like a paradox, but Sandler's observation is not self-contradictory. He meant that failure is part of the learning process—and that all true winners are out to learn and grow as they move forward in life.

Josh Seibert's exciting new book shows company leaders how to harness the natural adult-learning progression. It shows sales leaders (and others) how to create, support, and sustain a workplace learning culture that measurably improves performance. Josh knows, just as David Sandler knew, that launching such a culture always starts with top management's recognition that it is OK, even essential, for people to fail—within clearly defined boundaries that everyone understands.

Winning from Failing offers a proven roadmap for creating a high-performance learning culture in your organization, based on the principles of the Sandler Selling System® methodology. It's an important addition to the emerging, deepening discussion about how adults learn in the workplace.

David Mattson
President/CEO, Sandler Training

PROLOGUE

This Book in a Nutshell

A t Sandler Training, which I have been part of since 1999, we make our living helping sales teams. Many of the people we talk to are short on time. With them in mind, I've condensed this book's big ideas, which, I trust, will be invaluable not only to sales leaders but also to chief learning officers, presidents, CEOs, and human resources professionals. All of these people have a vested interest in compressing and maximizing the learning curves for sales managers and salespeople—and, ultimately, for everyone in the enterprise.

POINT 1: ADULTS DON'T LEARN THE WAY MOST THINK THEY DO

Adults learn differently from the way most people think they learn.

Exposure to Facts ≠ Learning

Sometimes leaders pretend that the simple exposure of their people to facts is synonymous with learning.

In the real world, adults don't learn by memorizing facts. There's a natural progression from acquiring knowledge, to the application in their role, to developing skills, and to adopting new habits. It looks like this:

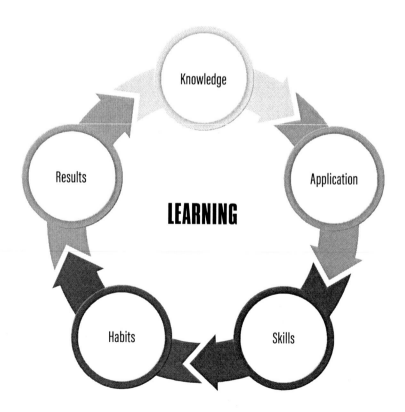

POINT 2: ADULTS LEARN BEST IN A LEARNING CULTURE

Whether they admit it or not, most books and "expert" training programs for adult learners work on the assumption that exposing adult learners to facts and then testing them on their retention of the facts is a path to mastery.

It isn't.

At Sandler, we believe that you have to create and sustain a learning culture that encourages people to attain new or different results and sustainable behavioral change.

Most books (this one included) are collections of knowledge. Some books assume that, once you know X, you can then go out and do X. That skips over the issue of whether or not a learning culture is in place.

This book won't tell you, "Here are the templates you have to learn. Memorize them, and your life will change." What it will do is help you get started on the challenging, long-term effort that results in an ongoing culture of learning.

This book and Sandler Training as a whole operate on the assumption that knowledge is just the beginning of the process—not only for salespeople but (more importantly) for the people who lead them.

Certainly, increasing knowledge will help, but it's not enough.

To create a space where it's safe to do something with what you've learned and the skills that you've acquired, to apply them in a different manner, to get a different outcome—that's the process you will explore here. That's what Sandler Training is all about. That's the reason we build our training and development strategies around the principle of long-term, ongoing reinforcement. It's not just because we want our clients to know our content precisely as it's written, but because it's necessary for the salespeople and managers we train to use that knowledge to change their behaviors and apply the ideas in a way that will create different results.

POINT 3: SUPPORTING A LEARNING CULTURE MEANS MAKING IT OK FOR PEOPLE TO FAIL

Did you have to read Point 3 twice, to make sure it really said what you thought it said? That's a common reaction to the idea that it's OK to fail. Many managers and executives demonize failure of any kind. This pressure creates the opposite of a learning culture; it creates a culture of fear.

Here's the reality about learning. Adults learn best when they fail within clearly identified, safe borders—spaces where it is OK to fail. In fact, that's the only way they learn, retain, and implement new skills based on behaviors that you want them to master.

Many managers misunderstand when we talk about making it OK for their people to fail. This book is not about letting people fail to do their job. Instead, it's about creating an environment that gives people a clear window of time or an environment within which they can apply something, fail without being punished, try again until they become more confident, eventually master the new behavior, and change the result to one that everyone wants.

Believe it or not, that's what always makes the difference in terms of team performance: the presence of a learning culture, supported from the top down, that makes it OK to fail within clearly defined boundaries.

POINT 4: START WITH MANAGERS

It surprises most organizations I work with to learn that their very best initial investment of time, money, energy, and attention is not to train the sales team. It's to train managers.

If this sounds counterintuitive to you, if you're tempted to fix the performance challenges you face by first training the salespeople, then I want you to know that I wrote this book for you. Know that you are not alone in feeling as you feel—and please do keep reading.

THIS BOOK

Consider this book a collaborative project between you and your coach. I'm going to play the role of the coach. In our coaching sessions—each exactly one chapter long—my aim is to support everything that needs to happen for you to produce the kind of learning culture that makes personal and professional breakthroughs possible.

Let's get started.

PART 1

How Hard Could It Be?

CHAPTER 1

To Change Results, Change the Culture

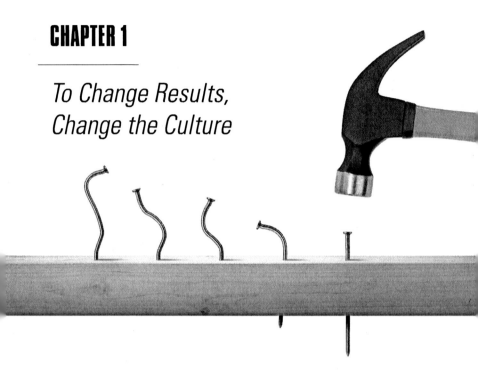

This book is about creating and sustaining a learning culture, the kind in which salespeople thrive even after the training is over. Creating that kind of culture takes action.

Simply reading the words on the pages and nodding in agreement, simply sharing the book with other people, simply asking people whether they read the book or got anything valuable out of it, will not deliver a change in your working culture. Guess what? Testing people in a written format to check whether they've memorized the content on these pages won't deliver a change in your working culture, either.

Let me be clear. If you're a manager, you must transform the experience of failure within the organization, and help people who report to you condition themselves to learn from failing. That means you must redesign the experience of failure within the organization, and, perhaps most importantly, condition yourself to learn from failing, to make it a cornerstone of your own plan for personal development. I call this "winning from failing," and it takes time and practice.

David Sandler, the founder of our company, created a revolution in selling. He did that by giving people the tools they needed to create both a different kind of working culture and a different selling routine. Both of those things—the working culture and the selling routine—were synchronized to match up with how adults learn and master new skills, new behaviors, and new outlooks on life. Sandler's message was pretty simple. If you want to change the results, you need to change both the working culture and the selling routine.

The reason is that most working cultures punish failure. Yours may do so in subtle ways you haven't even noticed. Helping you get better at noticing is one of the major objectives of this book. Let's start, though, by recognizing that you really do want a culture that rewards learning and growth. If you, like me, hold that truth to be self-evident, we're off to a good start!

"You have to learn to fail, to win."
—DAVID SANDLER

CHAPTER 2

A Dream Come True

When senior management at Prudential Financial said they wanted to promote me to sales manager in 1983, I figured my ship had finally come in.

My dream was coming true. I was going to be a major player. My agency had consistently ranked in the #1 or #2 spot in my region. I knew the business inside and out. I had seen others get promoted to such jobs—people who hadn't had the success in the field that I had. Prudential had finally gotten it right. There was every reason to believe that I could be a great sales manager.

I was the perfect candidate. I had started my own agency, and I had built it up to a substantial size in a relatively short period. I was a self-starter. I had hired some administrative help along the way, yes, but for the most part, I had gotten the business off the ground all on my own—as my agency's senior, and only, salesperson.

When corporate management told me they wanted to promote me, my chest swelled with pride. Who else would you want to pick to lead a sales team? Nobody, that's who! I had already built a successful agency from scratch. Clearly, I knew all the angles.

My district manager at the time told me that I would have no problem making the transition to management. This, he said, was the brass ring. As one of the top-performing insurance agents in the nation, I was about to catch it. He was proud of me. He wanted me to know I deserved this opportunity.

I couldn't have agreed more.

My district manager knew I wanted to expand my business. I could either keep developing my own business, with my money, or I could use Prudential's money to build a sales team and reap the rewards that way. One way or another, I was going to build an organization. The only question was whether Prudential was going to finance me.

It seemed like a pretty easy call. I told my district manager, "Yes."

He shook my hand.

"All you've got to do," he told me, "is show people how to do what you do."

HOW HARD COULD IT BE?

I signed on. I move my family from Charleston to Columbia, in South Carolina. I took over a new office. I got ready to tame the world.

There were twelve people on my new team. All I had to do, as my manager had said, was teach them to do what I did as an individual. How hard could that be?

Sure, these were people who had not reached their full potential, but that's why I was there. I talked to all of them. They were smart. Prudential didn't hire dumb people. They just didn't know how to do what I did. Yet.

I could tell they wanted to succeed. If I could just get eight or ten of those twelve people to come close to my performance levels, the team would be in great shape. We would be on top of the world in no time.

From the district manager's point of view, and from mine as well, it was just a matter of getting me to clone myself onto these twelve agents. My job was to turn each of them into a little Josh—by showing them how to do what I did. By gosh, that's what I tried to do. I worked my tail off, telling people what to do—assuming that, armed with that knowledge, they would start doing exactly what I had done when I ran my own agency. For some weird reason, though, it just didn't happen.

THE DREAM HEADS SOUTH

At that time, there were 2,500 sales teams within Prudential nationwide. When I started out, the team I had inherited had ranked number 1,863 in that network. Nothing but opportunity, right?

Six months later, five of my salespeople had left, and I had led my team right down into the basement. We now ranked at number 2,402. My business was in a free-fall. Something had to change, and it had to change in a hurry. But I had no idea what it was.

Here are some questions for you to consider before we move forward.

- Have you ever seen or experienced the situation where a "top performer" was assumed to be a "natural manager"?
- How "natural" did the person turn out to be in that role, in the short term, following promotion?
- What were the immediate results for the person promoted and the organization? Did stress levels go up or down? Did revenues go up or down?

> *"If there's a single lesson that life teaches us,*
> *it's that wishing doesn't make it so."*
> —LEV GROSSMAN

CHAPTER 3

You Can't Lose What You Never Had

lost a lot of people. I lost some sleep, too. I wasn't comfortable with the idea of seeing my team at the bottom of the Prudential heap. What was my turnaround plan going to be? That was the question that kept me up at night.

Of course, I didn't think ignoring my remaining team members was going to be part of that plan. The people who had stuck around were good salespeople, and they deserved the best support, advice, and coaching I was capable of giving them. I knew I had to do the very best I could with the people I still had on board. But I also knew I had to hire some new people to replace the folks I had lost if I wanted to have any hope of righting my ship. Not only that, I had to hire them quickly. There was no time for bad hires.

I asked myself a question: What kind of applicant did I need to target to hire someone who was likely to perform at or near the level at which I had performed, back when I was the only salesperson who mattered? The answer came back: Someone with a strong, proven, personal desire to succeed.

I decided that to fill my open slots, I would look for people with that kind of track record. My thinking went like this. If I could confirm applicants' claims to be strongly goal-oriented with something specific they had done to overcome some adversity in the past, if there was something I could document in their work history that showed that attaining goals really and truly mattered to them on a personal level, then maybe I stood a chance of making some decent sales hires. By "decent," I meant someone who would hit, or come close to, the income targets I set and stick around for a while.

I'm condensing a long story into a short chapter, but the bottom line is that this new approach got us out of crisis mode. Those new hires did, in fact, hit their targets and stick around, and my veteran team members did, too. We pulled it together. No one was performing at my level, but our numbers got better. We weren't at the very top of the heap, but we weren't at the bottom anymore.

But I still had a problem, a problem that took the form of a question I couldn't answer: Why couldn't I transform each of my team members into a Josh? Why couldn't I just show them what to do and expect them to follow along? Wasn't that supposed to be all I had to do?

Apparently not. Effective management, I now know, is not a matter of hiring the right people, showing them what to do, getting out of their way, and then gliding serenely, eagle-like above everything. I hadn't lost the ability to manage—I never had it. I hadn't even figured out what an effective manager was. I wanted to figure that out.

Change the people to change the culture.

CHAPTER 4

The Guys on a Submarine

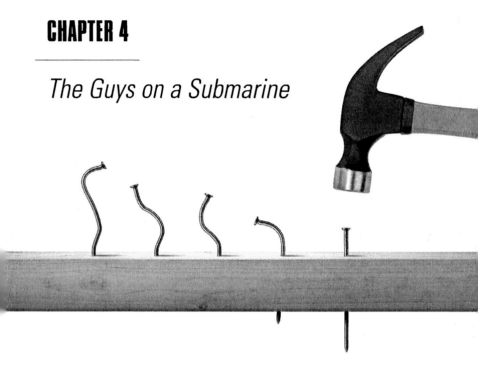

T hose go-getters I had hired at Prudential after I had nearly driven my office into oblivion did have something going for them, of course. What I discovered, although I didn't realize it at the time, was the "attitude" corner of David Sandler's famous Behavior/Attitude/Technique Triangle, also known as the Success Triangle.

You and I will be looking at that model in depth later in this book. But right now, I'd like you to take a brief look at the three sides of the Success Triangle. Those goal-oriented,

achievement-driven salespeople I brought on all had one of
the three corners down cold. They tended to see opportunity
in themselves, their situation, and their marketplace. Even big
challenges didn't get them down for long. They bounced back.

What was interesting was that even my recent achievement-
driven hires sometimes went into slumps. Occasionally, they
coasted, hit plateaus, or they became inconsistent. Over time,
I found even the people with great attitude got a little compla-
cent. Yes, I had hired enough of them to keep the office afloat,
but I realized that if all of them ever decided they were too
comfortable or if they all started easing off at the same time, my
office would start to sink—again.

That's when it hit me. I was now captain of a sales submarine,
yet I was surrounded by people I would never, in a million years,
have chosen to accompany me on an actual undersea voyage.
Attitude or no attitude, they were missing something. When I
realized what it was, my stomach started to turn.

You see, I had served in a nuclear submarine for the U.S.
Navy from 1974 until 1980. One of the things I learned during
that time is that, when you serve on a submarine, you are
putting your life into the hands of your crewmates every time
you descend below the ocean surface. Emergencies can and do
happen without warning. When they do, there is no time to pull
out a manual, issue remedial instructions, or hold someone's
hand. People not only have to know how to do their jobs, but

they also have to know how to do each other's jobs if that's what circumstances demand. Also, they have to be able to execute to perfection, instantly, every time, on instinct. Otherwise, you may never surface again, and that's not good.

I couldn't have put it properly into words at the time, but a kind of dread spread through my body when I realized that the guys who had been around me on a submarine were very, very different from the people I had on my sales team. The people to whom I entrusted my life on that submarine had a great attitude, and in that respect, the two groups resembled each other. But, those on the submarine had something else. Not only that, they did something else—something that no one in my office was doing.

They practiced—constantly.

Train your people to be able to execute to perfection,
instantly, every time, on instinct.

CHAPTER 5

Attitude Is Not Enough

To make it onto the crew roster of a nuclear submarine, you have to have more than the right attitude.

The right attitude helps. It's vitally important. But it's not enough. You have to be able to take over someone else's

job in a heartbeat and execute that job perfectly, from the first second onward—from muscle memory (also known as unconscious competence). There is no room for error. If something happens underwater and the crew needs to respond, there is no time for on-the-job training. You have to know what you're doing. If for some reason you don't, you're threatening the lives of everyone else on board, including your fellow crew members, specifically: me.

From my point of view, as your fellow crewmate, it doesn't matter how great your attitude is if, when there's a major problem below the surface, you a) don't know what to do, or b) haven't had extensive enough practice doing it.

If either of those situations exists, I don't want you on the submarine, and neither does anyone else. You're just too big of a risk.

These are the two big reasons that there are plenty of people who can and do perform superbly in other military settings but who simply don't make the grade when it comes to submarine duty. Even though their attitude may be great, their technique is still wobbly, and their behavior isn't yet second nature—isn't yet muscle memory.

To serve on a nuclear submarine, you have to embrace— and live—a working culture where you are constantly drilling, constantly training, constantly learning. In this culture—rare among military units—you're never finished learning. Let me repeat: You have to be able to take over someone else's job to a 100% efficiency level, instantly, which means you have to get used to going beyond your comfort zone. You have to make practice a way of life.

On this crew, drills are going on all the time. It's quite literally a matter of life and death whether one crew member has successfully ingrained the techniques and behaviors necessary to move from simply "knowing" how to do a job into "owning" how to do a job.

Owning the job means knowing what to do and doing it until it becomes second nature. That's a learning culture. That's a culture based on expanding and strengthening muscle memory. That's the kind of crew I worked on when I served on a nuclear submarine.

The men I had the honor of serving with had the right attitude, yes. But, they also had the right technique and the right behavior. Another point: They were never, ever satisfied.

Some of the crew on those submarines have been out of the service now for 15 to 20 years or even longer, but they still have the routine of "doing the drills." They're just drilling something else. They know that learning never stops—or at least never should stop. The ideal for these guys is that, when it's time to actually execute a skill, you don't have to stop and think, "What part of my training is applicable here?" It just happens. You just do it.

If you have to pause to ask that question during an emergency or when at battle stations on a nuclear submarine, you're probably already dead, and so is the guy next to you.

Why do I tell you all this? Because there came a point in my career where I realized that the model for adult learning I was using to recruit, manage, and retain salespeople needed to be based on all three parts of the Success Triangle: attitude, behavior, and technique. Attitude, as my experience in the Navy taught me, is not enough.

As it turns out, the U.S. Navy isn't the only institution saying that.

"Just Do It"

—NIKE

CHAPTER 6

The Sandler Success Triangle

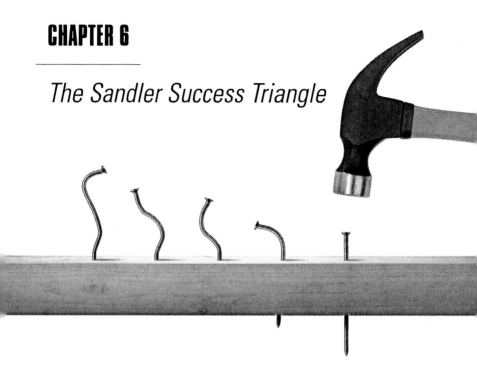

T he Sandler® Success Triangle, which I had never heard of when I first worked as a sales manager, was and is justly famous in the world of training and development. It has three points: behavior, attitude, and technique. As it happens, these are precisely the same three elements the Navy focuses on in developing people for the nuclear submarine program. The Navy doesn't use that language, of course, but that's what actually happens. You make quantum leaps in all three of those areas, or you don't make the program.

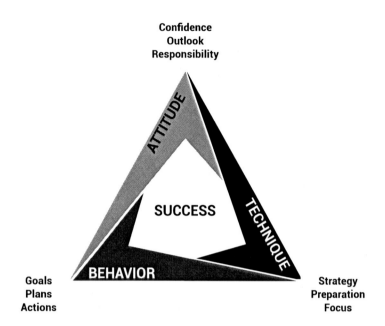

Confidence
Outlook
Responsibility

ATTITUDE

SUCCESS

TECHNIQUE

Goals   BEHAVIOR   Strategy
Plans   Preparation
Actions   Focus

Here's where I have to give you a little bit of background about how the Navy gets you ready to serve on the crew of a nuclear submarine.

There is a special institution dedicated exclusively to that purpose: the Naval Submarine School at the U.S. Navy base in Groton, Connecticut. All those who volunteer and are provisionally accepted to work on nuclear submarines have to go through Submarine School. That means you have to pass through a series of evaluations and exercises in which the Navy assesses your outlook on life, your capacity to contribute effectively to a team, and your overall psychological confidence, self-esteem, and self-image. That's one point of the Success Triangle right there: attitude.

But what about the other two? To answer that, I have to tell you a little bit about the way the Navy structures its drills for the people it has decided to place in Submarine School.

To prepare young volunteers for the rigorous demands of submarine service, Submarine School infuses sailors with the culture, esprit-de-corps, and, indeed, the behavior, attitude, and technique expected of every submarine crew member. For attitude, as I've suggested, the Navy closely evaluates each sailor's outlook on life, capacity for teamwork, overall psychological confidence and self-image. For behavior and technique, let's take a look at the way training is actually accomplished—how Submarine School prepares sailors for operating their ship while still in the safe confines of a land-based classroom.

Just as most military and airline pilots are afforded the chance to "fail" in a flight simulator (where a crash is humiliating but not fatal), submarine sailors are trained in shipboard operations, emergency situations, firefighting, and damage control in a maze of simulators. For example, there is a mock-up of a submarine engine room, with real pipes, valves, pumps, motors, and electrical panels. Several sailors will begin "standing their watch" in this simulator. Then, without much warning, water will begin to cascade into the space from various "broken" pipes. The sailors have to stop the flooding of very real and very wet water. It's loud; it's painful if you get in the path of the water stream; and frankly, even though you know nobody has ever died in the simulator, it's terrifying. As the water level rises up to the necks of the frantic trainees, they work ever more feverishly to "save the ship." Most trainees report that they forget they were in a simulator. They felt they were fighting for their lives. It's easy to fix the flooding when there's no pressure. It takes practice to fix it under duress.

If you fail in the simulator—and the odds are pretty good that you will—they shut the simulator off and eventually you get to try again. The good news is you didn't die. You can evaluate what you did wrong, go back, and try the simulator again. Pretty good deal, right? Time passes, you do drill after drill, and eventually you reach a point where you've actually mastered the simulator. Do they then put you on board, with sole responsibility for an engine room, and say, "Good luck," as the submarine heads off on your first mission? No. You haven't been tested in action. You've only been tested on the simulator.

Only after you've been through a whole bunch of simulators and learned a whole lot about submarines are you allowed to get on one. But you're not yet fulfilling a mission—you're still learning. Once you get on the submarine, you do the same kinds of drills you did in the simulator—only this time, you're doing it on a real sub. It's still a controlled environment. You're not responding to a real-life flooding situation, and there's still someone responsible for watching over you and qualifying whether or not you're ready to move on to a position of responsibility on an actual mission. You're still given room to fail in an environment where no one's life is actually at risk, and you're receiving close-correction supervision. There's a qualified person with you as you engage in those drills in that live environment. If you're about to do something dangerous, the person supervising you can intervene or stop the drill.

You repeat the entire process of simulation, practice, drilling, evaluation, and certification, until eventually, you graduate to being personally responsible for doing something on an actual mission. Even then, you still have to drill on a regular basis.

Consider these questions before moving ahead:

- Why do you suppose the Navy trains in that way?
- What does any of this have to do with the behavior and technique points of the Sandler Success Triangle?
- What, for that matter, does it have to do with the world of selling? Or any other activity people perform in the workplace?

Developing the right workforce through education and training
—FROM THE NAVAL SUBMARINE SCHOOL WEBSITE

CHAPTER 7

Practicing at the Wrong Time?

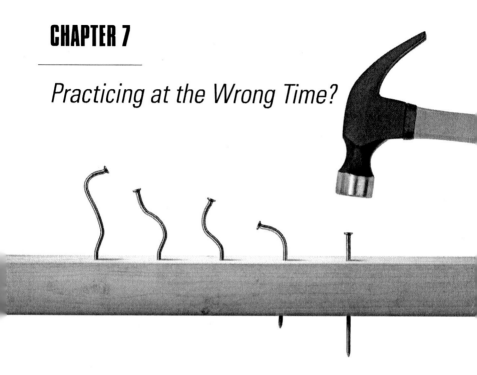

Look at the learning process again. In Submarine School, before you go out on a mission, you practice a whole lot before they even let you near a real submarine. Then, when they finally do let you practice on an actual submarine, there is always someone there to prevent disaster when you fail. The big surprise is, before you go out with the personal responsibility of performing a given task on a mission, they want you to fail.

You see, the U.S. Navy understands something that I hadn't quite grasped when I started my Prudential office.

They understand that the attitude point of the success triangle—the self-image piece, if you will—is not sufficient. The good people who designed the Submarine School realized that before you seal someone inside a metal tube and make him responsible not only for his life but the lives of everyone else on board, all three points of the Success Triangle (to use the Sandler terminology) need to be optimized. The Navy knows that the key to optimizing both the technique and behavior points of the triangle is failure—and not just any failure, but failure within a controlled-learning environment. Creating such an environment is the responsibility of the people in charge of making sure learning happens.

Let me be clear about this. When the U.S. Navy gives you a new technique to master, they not only expect you to screw up a couple of times as you implement it, they give you a safe environment in which to do so—an environment in which you are expected to fail—as part of the learning process. Why do they do that? Because time and experience have shown that the only way adults learn is by doing, and the only way adults get around to doing something at an acceptable level of mastery is by failing and trying again. It's just how human beings are wired. It's how humans acquire and improve what David Sandler called "technique."

Not only that, but once you master a specific technique, one that could conceivably mean the difference between life and death during a mission, the Navy cares too much about your life and the lives of the other people on board that ship to assume that what you've learned is forever. Even after you actually do get it, the Navy continues drilling that skill, over and over and over again, so that at the critical moment when you do encounter a situation where you have to perform, you don't have to think or try to remember what to do and how to do it. Muscle memory takes over because the learning has been reinforced. That's how to improve what David Sandler called "behavior."

Unfortunately, this is the exact opposite of what I was doing with my first sales team at Prudential.

Instead, I was showing or telling them what to do. I was penalizing them for failure when they got it wrong, which they inevitably did. I was also not drilling them before they went out on sales calls. The result was that they ended up practicing when they were in front of live prospects, the equivalent of a real submarine mission.

I was sending them out into a dangerous situation, after having read the manual to them only once. I was telling them to go out and execute the mission, after having promised them, in so many words, that they would be in trouble if they didn't execute properly. I did so having done exactly nothing to ensure that their technique and behavior were sufficiently developed to prepare them for the mission. I had let them down.

*Begin to create a controlled-failure
environment for learning.*

CHAPTER 8

Does This Ring a Bell?

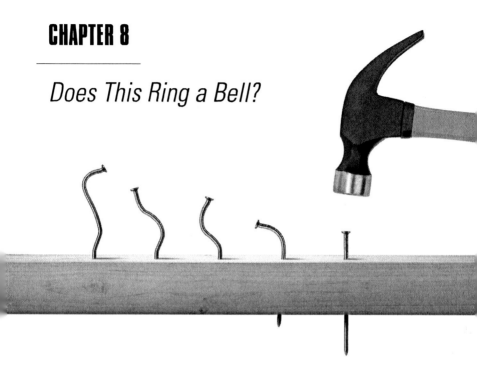

What I realized—what maybe some other managers responsible for sales teams have realized—is that simply telling salespeople what to do doesn't work.

That's not learning, and it's a mistake to pretend it is—not just for salespeople, but for anyone in the organization.

Learning is about optimizing performance. Sitting someone down and saying, "Next time around, just do what I did, and..." is not supporting the performance or the learning process. Again: It does not work.

Even if your intentions are good, telling doesn't work. Even if the technique you are passing along is sound, telling doesn't work. Even if your product/service mix is great, telling doesn't work. Even if you give people a written test afterward on what you've told them to do and they pass with flying colors, telling doesn't work. Even if you hire people with a good self-image and a positive attitude on life and work, telling doesn't work.

Why doesn't information transfer work?

Two reasons, and I hope you've figured them out by now. The first is that telling people what to do doesn't take into account how people acquire ownership of important new skills: through trial and error. If they don't have a safe place to apply a new tactic, fail at it, and try again, they will not attain mastery of that tactic. They will always go back to doing what they're comfortable doing instead.

The second reason is that just telling people what to do doesn't address their innate human need to grow and develop as people. People are wired to learn, but only in the direction that supports them in their unique growth path. People learn for their own reasons, not for anyone else's. The only reason people commit to improving their personal Success Triangle—their behavior, attitude, and technique—is that doing so connects to a goal that matters deeply to them on an individual level.

True confession: I didn't know what was important to each of the team members I started supervising at Prudential so it stands to reason that when I sat down to tell them something ("Next time around, just do what I did..."), they weren't all that invested in the discussion. Even though sometimes they nodded and said, "Sure," their behavior didn't change. They always reverted to what they were most comfortable doing, and the results were lackluster at best.

I have a feeling I am not the only executive facing challenges like this. Does any of this ring a bell for you, your team, or your organization?

If so, please keep reading. You're the person for whom I wrote this book. In Part 2, we'll move on from what doesn't work in terms of adult learning—and we'll start looking much more closely at what does.

TELLING ISN'T ENOUGH

Alice, a recently promoted-from-the-ranks sales manager, was just wrapping up a meeting in the conference room with her team when she got word from her assistant that she had a call from Sophia Larmar.

Instantly, Alice broke into a broad grin. Sophia had been Alice's biggest client before her promotion, and Alice knew what the call was about. "I'll take it right here," she called.

There was a brief moment of uncertainty from the team as the call was transferred. "Is the meeting over?" one of them asked.

"Nope. Watch and learn, friends," Alice told the assembled team. "I am about to close a 15-unit deal in record time. Mark my words. What you are about to hear is how sales is done."

Alice took the call and asked whether Sophia minded if she put the call on speaker. Sophia didn't mind. The team listened in, as instructed. Ten minutes later, Alice hung up the phone, looked around the room, and asked: "What do you think?"

The salespeople all smiled obediently. "Congratulations," said the most recently hired of the group.

"Thanks," said Alice. "Now let's get moving on those prospecting calls so you can all find your own Sophia Larmars!"

Everyone nodded. Alice clapped her hands and said, "Let's go!"

But as the meeting concluded and the salespeople left the conference room, Alice heard what sounded like grumbling.

The next day, Alice picked up through the grapevine that a few of the salespeople were complaining about what had happened at the end of the meeting. They thought the account should have been assigned to one of them. Alice couldn't understand why. What was she supposed to do when calls like that came in? Tell prime customers to deal with someone they didn't even know?

The answer? Yes. Then, facilitate the introduction personally. The first thing sales managers should do after being promoted from the ranks is to immediately turn over their client list to one or more salespeople. The clients should be properly informed of the change, and the sales manager should firmly redirect any sales calls or visits to the appropriate salesperson. No sales managers who wish to have a group of salespeople respect them should ever take any action that says, in effect, "I don't trust any of you enough to turn this over to you—none of you are good enough."

There's another important point to be made here. Alice had a great opportunity for a coaching moment—and she did not take advantage of it. Suppose she had used the conversation with Sophia to move the discussion forward—letting the team listen in—and had given credit for the sale to the right member of her team? Then suppose she'd asked questions like: "What went well?" "What could I have done better?" "What didn't happen that could have happened?"

Suppose, after that debrief discussion, Alice had then said to one of the salespeople in the room, "OK—now it's your turn. You make the next call. Let's see how it goes."

Instead of doing any of that, Alice put on her Superman cape and proved what a great salesperson she was. What message does that send to the rest of the team? "You queue it up—and I'll come in and close it for you." Nobody learns anything!

I've used this example because the world of sales and sales training is what I know best, but the underlying lesson is perfectly general. Every time you tell someone what to do and then swoop in to fix the problem when things don't go well, you are perpetuating a dysfunctional workplace culture.

Telling is not training.

PART 2

What Is Development?

CHAPTER 9

The Steps and the Staircase

A s you've gathered by now, I work with a lot of sales teams. I think I've heard just about every challenge and complaint there is to hear from managers and executives who face the same basic situation I did back at Prudential: getting a team up to speed. If I had to describe what I do with Sandler in a single sentence, it would be: Get the sales team to perform optimally by enlisting management to support, sustain, and reinforce a learning culture. (By the way, there have been plenty of situations where we've extended that culture throughout the organization, to departments that have nothing to do with sales.)

That doesn't happen instantly. In fact, the most common refrain I hear from managers and leaders who find themselves and their teams behind the eight ball is this: "Why can't you do this more quickly?"

In other words: "Why can't we hold a weekend training event, or a single-day intensive, or a half-day super-intensive, or a keynote speech, that will transform everyone overnight? Why can't we give people the new skills they lack, transform their attitude, and supercharge their performance in a matter of weeks, days, or hours?"

The answer most other sales training companies offer is the one that people most want to hear: "You can! All you have do is X." That's the implied premise of so many training programs. "Just give us a weekend and everybody will be changed." Or, "Listen to this audio for 30 days and you'll be fixed. (And you, too, can walk on hot coals!)"

Unfortunately, the real-world answer to why the change can't happen more quickly is: Your sales team members didn't get to where they are overnight, and no one has the mythical magic pill to change them overnight—not if you want to improve results and keep them improved for long enough for anyone to notice.

The hard, important truth is this: If you're going to get different results, you're going to have to get people to change the way they behave and perform. That's not going to happen overnight. It takes people a long time to reach the point where they are operating in a certain way, and it takes a while to change that mode of operation. It takes more than simply knowing what to change tactically.

It takes time. It takes support. It takes ongoing reinforcement.

TRAINING AND DEVELOPMENT

Let's take a moment to look at the difference between "training" and "development." People sometimes treat these words as though they are identical in meaning. They're not.

Training is a vital component of development. The problem is, most managers stop at training and don't complete the development cycle. There's a whole lot more to it, as you will see.

All too often, when people say "training," what they mean is to give an employee a shiny new toy to play with for a few days. A week comes, a week goes, and then some weeks pass, and maybe some of what has been "trained" sticks, but if that's all that has been done, the odds are that most of it won't. Usually, all that's left is another binder on the sales team's bookshelves and a memory of having played around with a new idea. That's not very effective.

Think of training as a step and development as the staircase. Learning is achievement that comes from the climb.

Development is the pathway to adult learning, the kind of self-motivated personal growth that results in a sustainable change in attitude, behavior, and technique and a corresponding sustainable change in performance.

A trainer shares strategies and demonstrates tactics. That's vitally important. But for the sales manager, the big disadvantage with training is that on its own, it doesn't change behavior in a positive way over time. Testing can measure information retention, but even if the test scores are good, that doesn't necessarily lead to sustainable positive behavioral change. Don't get me wrong. Training is a good thing. But if it's the only arrow in your quiver, you've got a problem. The ROI it delivers as a standalone event is typically negligible.

Development is more complex than training because it involves more than simple information transfer. It changes what's happening for the individual in a positive way, and the results of this kind of sustained change can be measured. It just takes a different approach than training alone.

THE DEVELOPMENT CYCLE

The development cycle is the kind of true learning that takes place as a result of an ongoing relationship in which someone with deep experience gives one with less experience time and attention and, in various ways, challenges that inexperienced person over time to overcome obstacles by expanding personal potential.

Appropriate professional training curriculum delivery is important. It's part of the development cycle. It's easy for most sales managers to do. Typically, providing training is within their comfort zone. However, being responsible for the development of another person often lies outside the comfort zone of the manager, and it requires a significant time investment. It requires cultural support for both the employee and the manager because development accepts as a working principle that it's OK to fail— and actually quite important to fail—if you learn something from the failure. Very often, working cultures are not set up in this way. When failure is punished, the development cycle suffers.

Changing this attitude toward failure usually constitutes a major cultural change. That cultural change is, in my view, absolutely essential. In this fast-changing era, only organizations that build and lead a corporate learning culture can count on delivering consistently high performance.

Early failure leads to earlier success.

CHAPTER 10

Going from Knowing to Owning

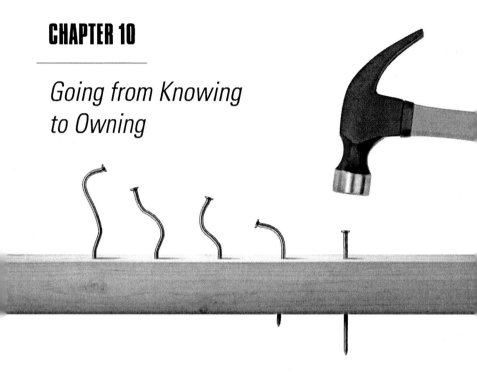

To have a learning culture, you have to focus not just on training but also on the ongoing development of the human being. For many organizations, this is a challenge. We at Sandler find in most corporations that there's a lot of emphasis put on training, specifically on training for new employees. The idea is to "bring them up to speed" and then leave them alone.

Often, this training takes the form of product knowledge, but it could also be training in processes and procedures relevant to anything that's happening within the organization. For salespeople, that's likely to include training in the company sales process: how to get to market, what the products do, how proposals work, and what company best practices are. Onboarding typically covers all of this.

The big problem with onboarding is that it usually translates to "a transmission of tactical information that stops shortly after the person is hired."

In a perfect world, aligned with a learning-centered culture, everyone would be onboarding all the time. However, that's not the world in which most people live. The world in which most live is one where management crosses off items on a list and then considers a new hire "trained."

SALESPEOPLE AND THE CHALLENGE OF "HERE'S HOW IT'S DONE"

For salespeople, onboarding usually incorporates an intensive period of "here's how we do it around here" data transmission. As part of the person's onboarding period, there may also be a ride along: direct experience on the front lines with a more senior person going out on a call with a real prospect. That way, the new hire gets to see "how it's done" in real time.

To be fair, companies who make this much of a commitment to training are in the minority. Most companies don't even go that far. Most just show the new hires a video or push them through a training program and assume that, since they can recite the right answers, they must now know the content. That's how managers convince themselves that new hires know what they're supposed to know. Cognitive learning is not enough, as the performance of too many sales teams proves. Yet a focus on that kind of learning remains the priority for most sales teams.

MOVING FROM KNOWLEDGE TO APPLICATION

There's nothing inherently wrong with cognitive learning. It certainly has its place. But in terms of developing people within a learning-based culture, it's only part of the equation.

From an organizational standpoint, you want to make sure employees do something with that cognitive knowledge. That means you want to support them in attaining a certain result by engaging in a certain behavior.

If your aim is to move to the next level, you have to help employees take that knowledge and quickly move toward a very different stage—toward the real-world use of that knowledge in their role. Applying something is very different from knowing it.

This is extremely important because, depending on what market they're asked to sell in or what industry they're selling to, the salespeople's knowledge needs to be applied differently. It will need to be applied very differently in a short sales cycle than it would in a longer one, for instance. Therefore, the learning process changes based on how they're going to apply what they know. That next level of learning beyond the cognitive level is called "application."

MOVING FROM APPLICATION TO SKILL

As salespeople begin to apply what they know differently in different situations, some of the things they learned and were tested on work quite well. They apply these things multiple times, and they become skilled very quickly. This learning process is yet another level called "skill."

One of the biggest reasons adult learners become skilled is often overlooked. They practice, and they fail.

In failure, they may learn even greater lessons than when they succeed. Failure leads to constructing boundaries and barriers that help people to refine and improve their performance. For instance, failure often teaches how much or how little of something needs to be done or how to adapt something from one situation to another.

Those lessons from failure cycle back into the cognitive level, becoming a new lesson to apply. The skill level follows that, accompanied by further refinements from additional failures, and the cycle continues for as long as people are learning and growing. This development cycle is how people develop different skill sets.

MOVING FROM SKILL TO HABIT

This constant refinement of cognitive knowledge is essential to adult learning because every prospect is different and every selling situation is different. As salespeople develop multiple skill sets relevant to multiple situations, they become more confident. With this confidence, they form the necessary habits that support them in each of the skill sets. This level is where performance becomes—or at least looks—natural. For lack of a better word, the salespeople "own" the skill set. They can do it almost without having to think about it.

This level involves muscle memory. People have practiced the skill and are successful with it enough times that expertise happens almost of its own accord. To an outsider, it might look as though someone who has reached this level is a "born salesperson." But of course, hundreds or perhaps thousands of trial-and-error sessions have preceded that level of mastery. A lot of work went into developing that muscle memory.

When it comes to learning, the human brain is the muscle that matters most. It requires constant conditioning. What causes skills to become habits is confidence—the kind of confidence that follows the successful application of the skill in the real world.

MOVING FROM HABITS TO RESULTS

The point at which you develop these habits is where you create sustainable behaviors. Cognitive knowledge is part of the process that creates the habit, but it certainly is not the only element.

Effective adult learning is creating a sustainable, productive behavior that wasn't there when you started or changing unproductive behaviors and replacing them with neutral or positive ones. Either of those outcomes is the typical result of a learning and development culture. Neither of those outcomes can take place as the result of a single day of training followed by a test. That won't sustain a behavior enough to result in consistently improved performance.

Look at the sequence again: knowledge, application, skills, habits, results. Those are the stages of an effective adult-learning model. Note that habit is the only stage that encompasses a lasting behavioral change.

WHY REINFORCEMENT?

The cognitive knowledge level is where most training programs are directed. However, if you want performance improvement, you can't stop there.

There's nothing wrong with a new tip, a new video, a new best practice. Those are all important pieces of the puzzle. But on their own, they don't lead to the development of the individual. That only happens with ongoing reinforcement within a learning culture. In other words, instead of being something one crosses off a list, development happens on an ongoing basis. It doesn't stop.

KNOWING TO OWNING

KNOWING ⟵——————————⟶ OWNING

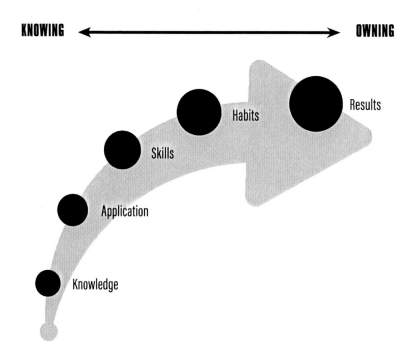

Results

Habits

Skills

Application

Knowledge

Your job as a sales leader is to create a learning environment that allows the knowing to owning process to happen—not for a week, not for a month, but for the entire employee life-cycle. Developing adult learners with this knowing to owning model in any one area includes supporting their overall personal growth, which can continue outside of the work environment.

THREE AREAS OF RESPONSIBILITY

The responsibility for development lies with three entities. First, it lies with the training organization, which must deliver relevant and applicable content that supports the knowing to owning process.

The training organization is responsible not only for good content and curriculum but also for good training methodology. Sandler uses group instruction because we have a very strong record of success with that method. There's virtue in training likeminded people among diverse industries in a group setting. You can share best practices and create a strong sense of mutual support.

Also responsible for the success of the training are the adult learners themselves. They are responsible for studying, completing the necessary action items, and having the sustained commitment necessary to move all the way from knowledge to habit.

Participants must be motivated to learn. If there is no personal desire to expand competencies or "go outside the comfort zone," then nothing will change regarding their development or performance within the role.

The third accountable party is management. Management is responsible for the culture. When I say management, I mean everyone from the direct supervisor working with the team to the senior leadership of the organization.

Management's actions and words either do or don't support a learning culture. In those instances where management accountability is lacking, it's often due to an inability to accept failure as part of the learning process. If the culture routinely punishes or stigmatizes failure without making allowances for failure as a learning experience, a learning culture simply will not take hold.

Very often, management embarks on a course of action that's believed to support the learning culture but then ignores evidence that the knowing to owning model is not being supported. Perhaps the most common example of this is when high-performing salespeople are assigned the task of showing lower performers how to do things instead of allowing the lower performers to practice and learn. Doesn't it make intuitive sense that if star salespeople are the only ones practicing in front of the group, they would be the only ones to get better?

By now, you can see why sitting a star salesperson down with a mediocre performer so the star can say, "All you have to do is this," will not change behavior in the lower performer in any sustainable, positive way.

Speaking personally, I learned that much at Prudential and have confirmed the point over and over again in the years since. The big difference for me now is a model that works far better.

Mastery is the process of going from
knowing to owning.

CHAPTER 11

The Missing Link

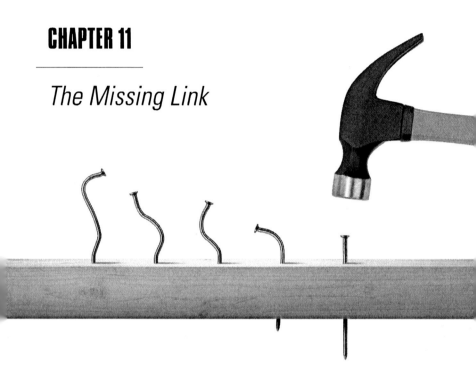

Giving people permission to fail is what makes a sustainable learning environment.

Learning, we must remember, is derived from experience—specifically, experiential application of new principles and tactics. You only learn when you apply, which is another way of saying that you only learn when you fail, adapt, and try again.

PERMISSION TO FAIL

By now, I think you can see that there's clearly a big difference between education, as defined by most organizations, and development. Education typically targets cognitive learning, and development relies on the experiential application of what has been learned cognitively—not just to support a short-term sales goal, but also to support personal growth in all areas of life.

If you think about your objectives as a manager during, say, the onboarding process, you may be very eager to educate your people about product specifications, or about company history, or about internal procedures you feel are important, or even about the sales process you believe to be the most productive. But until that knowledge is applied in an experiential way, until your team members have changed behavior in a way that supports both the individual and the organization, over the long term you aren't developing them as people.

For employees to learn and grow, leadership must create an environment that defines the boundaries within which they can safely accumulate experience by getting it wrong. In other words, you have to give them permission to fail in a way that doesn't threaten either their growth or the growth of the organization.

It's extremely important for a learning culture to allow for safe and even risky places, allowing both salespeople and managers to fail and learn. Real learning only happens when you apply what you've learned. The manager's job, far from eliminating risk, is to identify those places where taking a risk is safest and most appropriate (where neither the company nor the individual with the customers are going to be damaged) so people can engage in experiential learning and fail without fear of repercussions. The manager must clearly define the appropriate boundaries for failure. For example, "You can take any action between A and B. As long as you operate within those borders, failing won't be penalized here, nor will I swoop in to rescue you or do it for you."

THE BICYCLE

In discussing human learning, David Sandler used the metaphor of learning to ride a bike. Children don't learn to ride a bicycle overnight, nor do they learn to ride without significant failure along the way. They don't learn to ride a bike by watching a video. They don't learn to ride a bike by looking at a poster about riding a bike. They don't learn to ride a bike by being tested on memorized knowledge of what goes into riding a bike. They don't learn to ride a bike at a seminar.

They only learn to ride a bike by getting some coaching, getting on the thing, peddling, falling, getting some more coaching, getting back on, and peddling some more.

Here's the challenge. If parents (managers) feel the instinct to keep their children from falling, perhaps even to ride the bike for them, it only breaks and prolongs the learning process. By the same token, simply delivering the bike, wishing them luck, and walking away is not conducive to learning either. It will take them much longer to figure it out on their own. There's a middle ground of an optimized learning culture, and a lot of managers and organizations miss it.

True learning takes place when you create an environment where a person is supported and made to feel safe and protected—up to a point. True learning takes place in the space where your team members can accept your experience and your guidance, put on their safety gear, and try peddling between point A and point B.

They will fall. That won't always be easy for you to watch. In fact, it will be exhausting and even a little traumatic for you. But if you plan things correctly, they'll fall in a way that isn't catastrophic, and they will expand their capacity. They'll grow in confidence as they apply more and more of what you shared with them.

They have to own balancing, at an experiential level, for learning to occur. If you do nothing but lecture about the importance of keeping balance, you will waste your time.

If you only test on what "balance" means, you miss the point.

If you take them off the bike and try to ride the bike for them every time it looks like they're about to fall, you will lose and probably look ridiculous in the process.

Many sales managers will even fall into the trap of taking ten salespeople "off the bicycles" and trying to pedal all ten bikes at the same time. It's unsustainable. I know because I tried and failed at Prudential.

Setting up boundaries within which people can fail does not come easily to most managers. This brings us to the important but often overlooked topic of management development and managerial training.

Organizations usually focus their budgets and their attention on training salespeople. But from the perspective of creating and sustaining a learning culture, the development of the manager is at least as important—and probably more so. It's what makes permission to fail possible. It's the missing link between education of the salesperson and development of the salesperson as a human being.

FAILURE IS A STARTING POINT

As he pulled open the main office door of A1 Electro Mechanics, Yoshi, a salesperson, was not expecting much.

He was wondering whether he would be confronted with the classic, "Gee, I forgot you were coming in today," game from this evasive, difficult prospect. The three phone calls that had gotten Yoshi this far had been tough. First Scott, the CEO, had played hard to get, then he had pretended he had no money, and then, on the third call, he'd made noises about already having a supplier he loved—every trick in the book. Yoshi had earned this meeting, that's for sure, but he wasn't sure what would come from the first face-to-face discussion.

"Ah," Scott said, greeting Yoshi after a wait of just a few minutes. "You must be that persistent salesperson who doesn't take 'no' for an answer."

Momentarily at a loss for words, Yoshi was stunned by the CEO's appearance. Scott's Grateful Dead T-shirt had rips in it, and, though it was clean, old grease and dirt stains were still visible. His jeans had holes in both knees. Yoshi could not stop staring at the huge gold earring and the long silver ponytail.

"Surprised you, didn't I?" Scott asked. "Expecting a three-piece suit and a pair of wingtips, maybe?"

"Well, you certainly don't look like you sounded on the phone."

"What's that supposed to mean?"

"I guess you sounded like someone who is in charge," Yoshi said. The moment the words left his lips, he knew the meeting was over. It hadn't come out the way he wanted—and now it was too late.

"I am in charge," Scott said. "Tell you what. Since you don't think I'm in charge, turn around, head out of the door, and find someone else in the company to talk to."

Yoshi turned and walked back out to his car. "Man, did I screw that one up," he thought to himself.

But instead of driving off, Yoshi sat in his car and began mentally reviewing his approach to Scott, starting with the very first phone call. He asked himself: "What could I have done differently?"

He spent the next half hour in the parking lot writing down good answers to that question.

Point to ponder: If you have failed and you know why you failed, you are 99% closer to increased success. That's not just true for salespeople. It's true for managers, as well.

Developing salespeople necessitates
the development of managers.

CHAPTER 12

The Four Roles

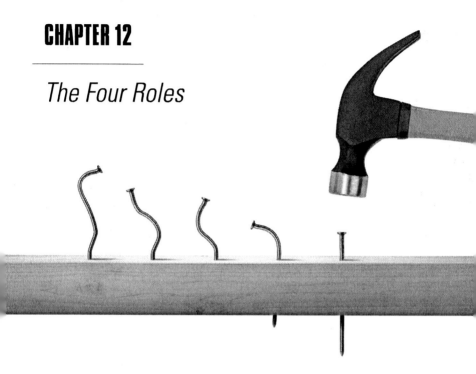

Permission to fail—within clearly defined borders—is essential to development. When it comes to salespeople, there is a special challenge to consider. Failing within the role called "salesperson" often entails hearing the word "no." Salespeople often feel emotionally conflicted from the experience of hearing "no." Therefore, they are likely to miss the lesson learned—whatever that lesson might be. Typically, they miss the lesson learned because they are busy going through the following stages, which David Sandler identified as the Anatomy of a Failure:

- **Disbelief.** Your mind will deny what it can't accept. The first step after failure is head-shaking: "I can't believe this happened to me."
- **Fear.** Fear is a useful tool if you understand it. Fear is a survival mechanism. It gets your juices running.
- **Anger.** You think the world is crumbling, and you get angry.
- **Acceptance.** You accept responsibility for your failures. You're getting back in touch with feelings and reality.
- **Despair.** Reality has returned, despair comes with it, and you are uncomfortable about that.

This is a very emotional process. Only the fourth stage—which a lot of salespeople don't reach on their own—carries the potential for personal growth. Unless there is a coaching method in place, the salesperson never gets to the lesson learned. Instead, the salesperson does the same thing over and over. (By the way, there are similar emotional issues and challenges associated with hearing a "yes" answer from a prospect.)

Selling is unique because it's such an emotional roller coaster. The emotionally demanding nature of this job brings us to the four essential roles of the sales leader—which differ in important ways from how other leaders in the enterprise fulfill these roles.

Coaching is one of those core responsibilities. For the sales leader, coaching is all about helping salespeople successfully navigate the emotionally difficult stages so they can get to the point where they can learn and grow—and develop themselves as sales professionals.

WE ALL NEED SOMEONE

The Rolling Stones may have said it best: We all need someone we can lean on.

If experiential learning is going to happen, there has to be a coach to help salespeople deal with the emotions of either the *yes* or the *no* answer. There has to be someone to help them turn either situation into a learning moment. It's quite difficult—very nearly impossible—to do on your own. Some sales masters can figure it on their own, but they're few and far between and it still typically takes longer. Everybody needs a coach.

However, instead of coaching, many managers go into Critical Parent mode. Managers are tempted to say, "Here's what you did wrong; here's what you should've done." It's because they took on the responsibility of being a supervisor before they learned how to be a coach. Knowing how to be a good coach doesn't come automatically just because you are named manager.

Most sales leaders are never taught how to be effective coaches. Why? Because management says, "We're going to invest in the sales team," yet there's no effort (or budget) set aside to develop sales managers. As a result, the company ends up treating the symptom most of the time, instead of the real problem.

Of the millions spent on sales training, how much do you think is spent on retraining people who didn't get it the first time?

Typically, only 10% of the content actually sticks. Even then, it only sticks because it's comfortable and already part of a person's habits. People rarely willingly go outside of their comfort zone, and there is no ongoing reinforcement designed to encourage them do so. For managers, there is no training in how to provide that coaching.

THE FOUR ROLES

As I've suggested, four roles are essential for managers to help their sales teams find success. Yet, managers typically only perform one of them.

The **supervisor** role, which is what most managers fall back on, includes: oversight, monitoring data, and corrective input.

The **training** role is where the manager identifies and ensures the team is trained in skills that support development. The trainer does not have to be the manager, but the manager needs to make sure that training happens.

The **mentoring** role is where managers demonstrate best practices. They make sure the salesperson experiences, on a personal level, "how it's supposed to be done." Again, the person filling this role may or not may not be the manager, but the manager must make sure it happens, by, for instance, pairing up a new salesperson with a top performer. A challenge arises when what the manager does in the way of mentoring doesn't match up with what the training is supposed to be. The mentor's behavior speaks louder than manuals or posters.

In the **coaching** role, managers provide a supportive learning environment. They give the person permission to fail within predetermined borders. They support development of the employee as a person. They help the person work through emotions so that he can get to the lessons that need to be learned in any given situation. *NOTE:* Coaching is not the same as rescuing, which is a cycle that leads to dependency.

If the members of the sales team are to grow and develop, all four of these roles must be fulfilled. In the next chapter, we'll take a closer look at why that typically does not happen—and what the consequences are for the organization.

Everyone needs a coach.

CHAPTER 13

Beyond Mighty Mouse

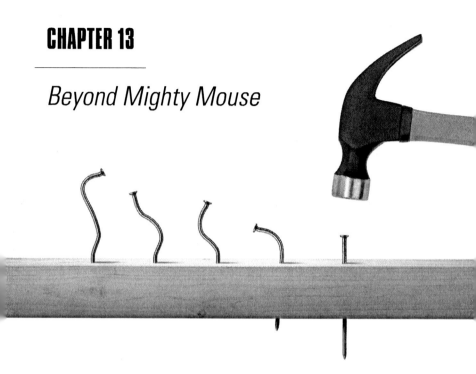

The learning culture, a culture where failure is celebrated within certain clearly defined borders, doesn't emerge in most sales teams. To solve the problem, we must look at a sensitive topic: how sales managers get hired.

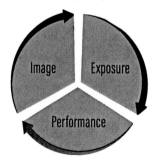

Typically, there are three factors that strongly influence the hiring of a given sales manager. They are:

1. **Performance.** The person emerged as a top salesperson in the organization.

2. **Image.** The person looks and sounds like other sales managers or important figures within the company.

3. **Exposure.** Key decision makers, liking what they see about this person, agree the person should become a sales manager.

Usually, there are two of these factors at work when hiring a sales manager. Sometimes, all three are in play. But notice that there is no bullet point in the list above for competency.

Typically, as a result of these three stars aligning, the promoted person has a low competency for the role. The four leadership roles mentioned in the previous chapter are not second nature. In the vast majority of cases, sales managers begin the job the way I did—without any clear sense of what the ideal skill sets for salespeople are or what steps should be taken to develop them.

As a result, new managers typically do a lot of telling, showing, and closing. When people don't perform the way they did, they end up taking on a lot of the work themselves, telling themselves, "What choice do I have? We need to hit the numbers."

Six months later, they are telling themselves something very different: "If I just made this much effort as a salesperson, I'd be making a lot more money!" Many realize that they are now working twice as hard for half as much income. What happens next? They decide to go back into sales. (Or burn out. Or get fired.)

Why does this happen? Because the person who has been hired into the managerial position is missing three of the four skill sets necessary to do the job. Typically, this person is competent in the supervisory role, but not involved at all in training, mentoring, or coaching people to have moments of experiential learning.

In fact, when a salesperson on this manager's team fails, that's likely to become a big political and interpersonal problem, not a moment of learning at all. Failure prompts the manager to put on a Mighty Mouse cape and shout, "Here I come to save the day!"

THE PARADIGM SHIFT

The problem is not that managers are incapable of being good sales leaders, but rather they are underdeveloped at the job of developing others.

At the end of the day, if you're doing the job, you have to get production from the team. You can't be out in the field for them. People need to be trained and reinforced over time in mastering the skills necessary to do it themselves. This requires a paradigm shift—a big one!

For example, salespeople must be supported as they make the transition from a fear-of-*no* mindset to a mindset where they actively seek out the *no*. For most salespeople—and, let's face it, most sales managers—this is a new and unfamiliar idea. At first, it may even seem a little threatening. Let's explore this in the next chapter.

> *Your company must be as committed to the success*
> *of its managers as it is to its own success.*

CHAPTER 14

The Paradigm Shift

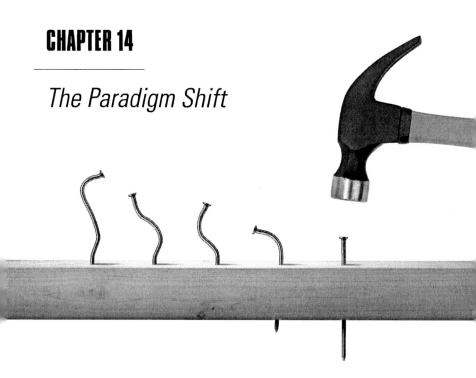

I f you are going to have a learning culture, then you have to have certain things in place. As I think you can see by now, one of the things you absolutely, positively, have to have is a competent manager who is capable of fulfilling all four roles of the job. For most organizations, this is essential to the creation and maintenance of a supportive learning culture. If the manager happens to be leading a sales team—as most of the managers I work with are—the four roles must be approached with special care and a clear understanding of the gaps that may have inhibited learning in the past.

As we've seen, most sales managers are hired without any direct assessment of their skills and capacities in fulfilling the four critical roles of this position. Typically, they got their ticket into management because of their productivity as a salesperson, their image, and the degree of exposure they received within the organization. Once those three boxes were ticked, people stood back and said, "Go get 'em, hot shot!" What I'm proposing is a direct challenge to that model.

I'm proposing that you take some time to figure out whether candidates for the manager job have been productive through other people, as opposed to being personally productive. That's the essence of sales leadership: to get productivity flowing through others. It's not easy to do. Most salespeople are not well-equipped to do that.

If they're already in the position of sales manager and they don't have the capacity to get sales productivity from their people, then you have to equip and support them so that they become able to do so.

THE MOST CHALLENGING PART

Here's the most challenging part of this paradigm shift. Getting managers up to speed so they're capable of fulfilling the four roles of supervisor, trainer, coach, and mentor is, strategically speaking, more important than training the sales team to do anything.

I realize this is a counterintuitive idea to most decision makers. But it is true. The managers you have on board who haven't yet mastered the job description of being a sales manager are the ones you need to train first—before you train the salespeople.

I'll be expanding on this critical point in later chapters of this book, but here I'd like to offer an example that hearkens back to my experience in the Navy.

Many people join the Navy as enlisted personnel, and some of those enlisted personnel raise their hand up high and shout "Yes!" when asked whether they want to become officers.

Now, if you happen to be one of those people who said, "Yes," I will grant that you have made it clear that you want to become a leader in the Navy. Who knows? You might even have what it takes to become a leader.

But, even if you are the highest-ranking enlisted person on the ship, until you apply for, gain entry to, and complete a course of study at Officers Candidate School, you're not going to be given the responsibilities of a naval officer.

That's the way the Navy operates when it comes to getting people ready for duty as leaders. When it comes to getting sales managers ready for duty as sales leaders, I believe you should operate your organizations in much the same way.

First invest in management development.

CHAPTER 15

The Radical Proposition

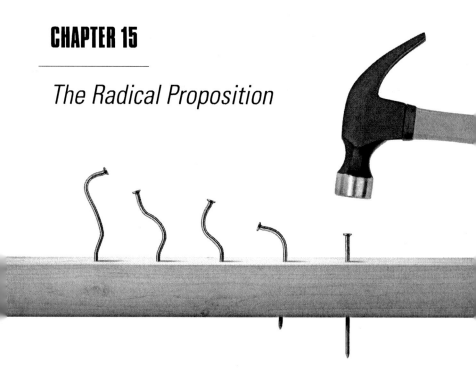

F rom what we've been discussing, you know that encouraging a shift has to do with how you train and promote managers. You know that management hires are typically made by performance, image, and exposure, and you also know that those factors typically lead to mismatches and problems with organizational culture.

I want to make a radical proposition in this chapter, one that starts with what you know and moves you forward—that moves you beyond your current comfort zone.

Before I present that radical proposition, however, I invite you to consider some cold, hard facts.

First, when it comes to sales professionals, including sales managers, many are engaged in what I call "spaghetti recruiting and promoting." As in, "throw it against the wall and hope it sticks." Until it's ready, that noodle will slide to the floor.

Second, the spaghetti approach doesn't work. It always leaves one or more gaping staff holes to fill. All too often, the response is more spaghetti recruiting and promoting. "Hey—here's some-body. Let's fill that hole with this fellow Innocent Bystander. He looks good; he's got a good resume; he seems to wear the same clothes most of us do. No problem. We've got the guy!" There's no check for competence, no benchmarking. Nothing is done to groom for competency. Those hiring are distracted by the exter-nals. This leads to an endless cycle of burnout and turnover—not only among managers but also among salespeople.

At Prudential, our turnover rate of salespeople was grim. It wavered around something like 90% over four years. Over that time, we were investing close to $200,000 in each hire. There was a multitude of reasons for the turnover. My point is, our industry accepted that. Our goal was to beat a retention rate of 10%. If we'd found a way to get up to 13%, there probably would have been a round of banquets and awards.

The retention among managers was typically even worse than that among the salespeople. People decide to move on when they realize they can't sustain a department's level of performance or don't want to. Quite a few decide they've picked the wrong career path. They're usually right about that. They realize there's no structure there to support and develop them. So, they go into fight-or-flight mode. Mostly managers flee, one way or another. It's just a question of which direction: up, down, or out.

Third, sales managers are in denial about the impact that flinging spaghetti has on the overall organization. Many companies and industries have numbers like the ones we had at Prudential. Most of their leaders say things like, "It's always been that way." There's always a succession of gaping holes. There's always a mess for someone else to clean up.

My radical proposal, based on what you already knew and what I've just shared with you, is that when it comes to sales management, you must, first and foremost, make an organizational commitment to stop throwing spaghetti at the wall. You want to develop and rigorously pursue a methodical hiring process. You want to make an explicit organizational commitment that your first stage in filling any sales management vacancy will be to identify the right candidate for development. You also want to confirm that it is only after you have developed a candidate that you will promote to the role of manager.

I want you to hold off on your next attempt to promote a salesperson to management, at least until you have finished reading this book.

For most organizations, this is a difficult commitment to make and implement. There is a learning curve. But rising to the challenge, as you will see, carries immense competitive advantages.

Think strategy and structure
before staffing and skills.

CHAPTER 16

Two Kinds of Managers

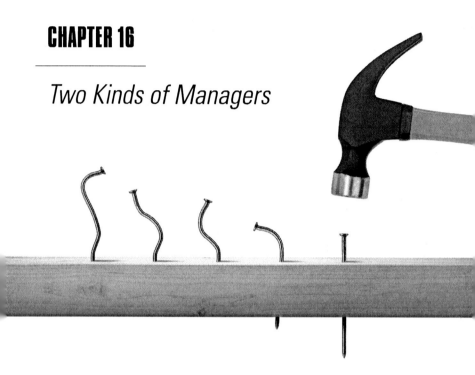

I n any discussion of sales management, there comes a point where you have to acknowledge that there's a huge difference between line management and staff management.

The line position is in the field. This line manager is the one who is accountable to senior management for revenue, profit, and the overall performance of the team. There is also likely to be a director-level individual (such as a vice president) or someone in a staff position who supports sales. That's staff management. When someone is personally accountable for results, that's line management. Both are important when we talk about coaching.

In the case of the sales team, your line manager is your field manager. That's the person who's out there supporting development and coaching salespeople in the field. Staff management, by contrast, would be people like Sandler trainers and coaches. These leaders are disconnected. They're not personally accountable so they can be a little bit more objective. They're not emotionally involved in the sale.

It's often difficult for line managers to be objective because they're the ones in the field with the salesperson. They're working day to day, and they can give immediate, direct feedback based on personal observation. It's important to have that. But the downside of this is that if those managers are personally accountable for getting results, there is a danger that they might slip into "rescue" mode, particularly if they have a personal history of being a successful salesperson.

Often, they fall into the previous role or become subject to the emotional drive, and their coaching role recedes. In its place are justifications like: "Yeah, but we need to close this deal." Or, "Yeah, but it's the week before the quarter ends and we need better numbers." Or, "Yes, I know I need to coach and develop my people, but that's a long-term objective. This is a special situation, and I have to handle it in the short term and intervene. I'm feeling pressure to get results this week because the vice president's coming to town, and I want the numbers to look good."

This example is how managers step around the good, solid coaching that allows the salesperson to learn from failure. This is the part of the job that is most likely to be underdeveloped when the person is promoted into management.

This pattern is so common that it's important to acknowledge there is a risk to only having one manager in the picture. You need both a line manager and a staff coach.

The most effective staff coaches are trainers—people who can provide the objective, distanced coaching because they are not emotionally attached to the results (unlike the line manager). Trainers can be much more objective when it comes to developing an individual, whether it's a manager or a salesperson. They can stay in the role of coaching, training, and developing.

Both the field manager and the line manager are important. If you could just have one, you would want a line coach who is very schooled in the Sandler system such that he would not flip into rescue mode whenever a salesperson faces a problem. That would be ideal. Until that development happens, until your line manager has the emotional balance to withdraw and not get emotionally involved in the sale, you probably need two people.

That's why management development, with a detached coach, is so important. It's comparable to golf. The coaches for the world's best golfers are not emotionally attached to the outcome of the tournament. They aren't on commission. If the golfer wins, they don't get a bonus or an override, and if the golfer loses, they don't take a hit.

So if that's the staff manager, who is the top golf player's line coach? You guessed it: the caddy. These caddies, at this level, are brilliant coaches. The best ones have known the golfer for quite some time. They have all kinds of experience, and they usually know the right thing to do. They can talk with the golfer about what's about to happen. They can debrief after the shot.

What's great about the world of golf is that the caddy is prohibited from getting onto the green and taking a shot. That's a little different from what usually happens in the world of sales, but it's a good reminder of the way things ought to be. You don't want the line coach jumping onto the green, grabbing the golf club, and saying "I'll handle this putt, Tiger."

Before we move on to Part 3 of this book, in which we'll look at the best ways to move away from the "I'll handle this putt" mentality, I'd like to sum up the big idea of Part 2 for you, using our golf metaphor.

In golf, to the degree that the caddy is out there swinging the golf club, it's a dysfunctional relationship. The same is true of the relationship between the line manager and salesperson.

For objective, unemotional guidance, find
a coach on whom you can rely.

PART 3

The Critical Distinction

CHAPTER 17

Stepping Out of the Drama

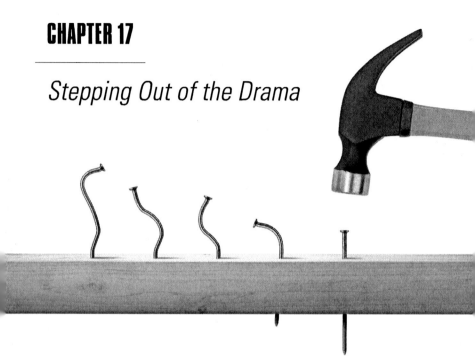

A critical distinction I want you to try on for the rest of our time together is that people in general, and salespeople in particular, only grow within their workplace role when they accept personal responsibility for that growth.

You can't do it for them. Salespeople need to discover for themselves how and why to become personally accountable for growing within the job and executing the sales process.

The first tool I want to share with you to help you distinguish between whether you're helping or hurting your team members' chances at taking responsibility for their own success is the Karpman Drama Triangle. Transactional analysis pioneer Stephen Karpman came up with this triangle to describe a kind of game that human beings play with one another. Sales managers may not think of themselves as playing games with their salespeople, but I am here to tell you that, if you're not careful, you can get sucked right into it. This particular game, which is all about manipulation, is a particularly destructive one.

Take a look at Karpman's model (below) and ask yourself whether you've ever found yourself playing it—whether any part of it seems even vaguely familiar. If your answer to either question is "yes," then you—like me, like most sales managers—have, at some point, with one or more members of your team, been entrenched in manipulation.

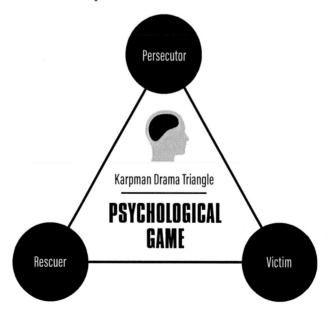

This game, as you can see, has three players: persecutor, rescuer, and victim. I know I've played all three roles during my career, and I'm willing to bet that you have, too.

Sales managers can be victims very easily, whether or not they choose to say that word out loud. It happens anytime a manager has said or thought, "Woe is me; I don't have the best salespeople; I'm handcuffed because I have low-level performers like Carl on my team. If only I had the players Julia has, in the office across town, I would do a lot better."

Enter the salesperson. Now the sales manager turns into the persecutor. "Carl, if only you were performing better, this department would be in a lot better shape."

Five minutes later, he can be the rescuer: "You can't do well, Carl, because you are new. Step back and I'll show you how it's done."

Did you notice, though, that in none of those roles does the manager accept any accountability for creating an environment in which growing and developing salespeople is possible?

In all three of those roles, the manager discourages employees from taking personal responsibility for the learning process. In the first, the manager doesn't accept the members of the team as they are. In the second, he makes them feel bad for failing. In the third, he grabs the golf club, steps onto the green, and says, "Stand back, Tiger—I'll handle this putt."

Here's the secret when it comes to the Drama Triangle. The only way to win this particular game is to choose not to play.

You can't ever win if you play the game inside the triangle, and neither can your salespeople. The roles bounce around, everybody plays different roles, and people jump into the roles they like best to deal with different situations. But nobody learns anything. Nobody grows.

The only way to win the drama game is to step outside the Drama Triangle.

Don't play the game.

CHAPTER 18

"No Drama" Takes Some Practice

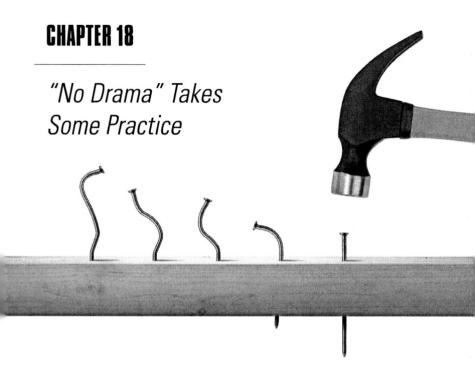

O ften, when I tell groups of managers about the Drama Triangle, there is a certain despair. People get very quiet. People wonder what comes next if they have to find a way to avoid being a victim, being a persecutor, and being a rescuer. One manager took a deep breath, sighed, looked me in the eye, and said, "Josh, I don't know how I'm going to pull this off. I just thought of my most recent work day. I spent my whole day in that Drama Triangle."

My response is always the same: It takes practice to learn to step out of the Drama Triangle. It doesn't happen when you stick with what's familiar to you. It doesn't happen overnight. But it can happen, and the sooner the practice starts, the better off everyone is.

No one—not salespeople, not sales managers, not anyone else with a pulse—is ever truly outside the triangle's influence. Disabling it and shutting off the energy to it is the work of a lifetime. It's an endless loop. No one ever breaks free from it completely. But some people are a lot better at recognizing what's happening than others, and noticing what's happening is where the change must begin.

If you don't notice what's happening, you may find yourself bouncing between the roles of victim, persecutor, and rescuer. Look how easy it is for a salesperson to manipulate a manager by becoming the rescuer: "You know, just between you and me, you really are a great sales manager—much better than the vice president gives you credit for." The salesperson is making the manager emotionally attached to feeling better about himself by putting down the VP. This puts the manager in the victim role so the salesperson can rescue him emotionally.

The longer you play in the triangle of blame/helplessness/rescue, the less development happens. The only way to win this game is to decide not to play. That takes practice. It takes noticing what's going on.

Disengaging from this manipulative game takes a certain competency. It involves control of one's emotions. That's a very important competency, and it doesn't come naturally. It's particularly important in management. Managers have to have control of their emotions because, in the real world, salespeople are often emotionally out of control. When salespeople get out of control, that's when dangerous things happen in a sales call. The coach has to be the one who brings salespeople back from that brink of excess emotion.

Remember that example I shared with you earlier of the caddy? The caddy's role is to keep that golfer on an even emotional keel, to keep the golfer stable. Although the caddy can, of course, offer suggestions on what the golfer could be doing, the critical part of the role is to keep the golfer emotionally in control of the situation.

On the range, during practice time, that's when the caddy can offer advice to the golfer on how to swing. But when they're out in the middle of a tournament, the job is very different. That's when the emotional swings can take all the skills the golfer has developed and just throw them away. The caddy's #1 job during the tournament itself is to help the golfer's emotions to stay even and manageable.

Whenever sales managers stop noticing what's going on, whenever they lose control of their emotions, the triangle takes over. One of those three roles—victim, persecutor, or rescuer—is going to emerge. But as you get better at noticing when these roles start beckoning, you develop the critical competence of emotional control.

DON'T RESCUE THEM!

As Juan, the veteran sales manager, walked across the hotel lobby after a Lions Club meeting, he happened to see Briane, a major local manufacturer, talking to one of his new sales hires, Kyle Rookie.

Briane and I go way back, Juan thought to himself. *Actually I think she was my very first sale, way back when.*

"Juan," called Briane, as she saw him from across the room. "Come on over. I've been beating up on Kyle here. How the heck are you?"

Juan came over and shook Briane's outstretched hand. "Pretty good," he replied. "Sales are up, good product, good people." He nodded toward Kyle. "What more could a guy want?"

"Well, tell you the truth, there is something that you want that you don't have yet," replied Briane, putting her hand on Juan's shoulder.

"And that would be?" asked Juan, his voice trailing off.

"You have to ask? You want me to buy today, just like I've bought from you for the past..." Briane looked up at the ceiling for a moment, then said: "What's it been, 20 years now?"

"More like 25," replied Juan.

"Loyalty like that must be worth something. Listen, Kyle and I can't seem to come to an agreement on price. You know me, Juan. I've always been a hard bargainer, and all I ever wanted all these years from you was a fair price."

"Briane, I think you and Kyle can work that out."

Briane shook her head slowly.

"Juan, hate to put it this way, but that new place two towns over just gave me an unbelievable price this morning, and they don't even know me. Doesn't loyalty mean anything anymore?"

Juan looked at Kyle and then at Briane. Juan felt pretty important at that moment.

"Look," said Juan, his eyes level with Briane's, "how about you and I head to my office and work on—we'll call it a special 'loyalty price.' If you are satisfied, you can come back and give Kyle the go-ahead. He's still the salesperson of record for this deal."

"Sounds good to me," replied Briane.

"Sounds good to me, too," said Kyle.

"OK, now that the two of you agree, let's go, Briane. Let's put our heads together like in the old days."

As the rookie Kyle watched the two successful business people head out the door and toward the parking lot, he thought, *Juan and I ought to double team more often!*

POINT TO PONDER

Management's role is, in large measure, about helping people learn. What was learned in the story above?

Unfortunately, the main takeaway was: Whenever a sale is in trouble, Kyle can count on Juan to rescue it for him.

Juan stepped in and saved the sale for Kyle. It made him feel good to do that. While Kyle no doubt appreciated getting credit for the sale, he learned the wrong lesson—and Juan let his desire to be "important" play too big a role.

*Emotional control is a critical competency
within the manager's role.*

CHAPTER 19

Lead with Management

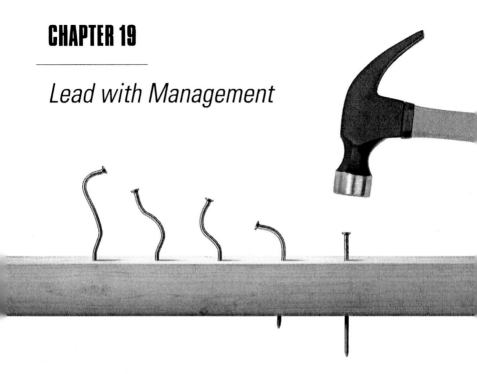

Because we're in the training and development industry and we're known primarily as sales trainers, we at Sandler get hundreds of requests every year from executives asking us to train their salespeople.

But there's a surprise waiting for most of these decision makers. We turn almost all of those requests down. We make every effort not to train salespeople until everyone in management has been trained in the Sandler Selling System.

It's ill-advised—and quite rarely done—to train salespeople

without involving, at a minimum, sales management. More often than not, we start with management training well before implementing sales training. Why? Because if development is to be sustainable, it's crucial to have management coaching in the field. You just can't coach from the Drama Triangle, which is where most managers have learned to spend the majority of the working day.

No organization can develop salespeople over the long term that way. Developing salespeople is the name of the game. It's the crucial distinction on which organizations stand or fall.

If you have to lean one way or the other, the best possible choice is to lean into management when it comes to organizational development. Otherwise, you are going to find yourself stuck in the drama, and, by extension, stuck in the "my way or the highway/here, let me do it" model of sales management (if you can call that sales management).

The message here is pretty simple, which is why this part of the book is short. Management has to lead the way, and it has to eat its own dog food. If the objective is to have sustainable income growth on the sales team as the result of sustainable positive behavioral changes, you must get management committed to developing individual salespeople on both a personal and organizational level. If you expect to create sustainable sales growth without that, you're placing your money on the proverbial long shot. The odds of success for delivering sustainable positive change on the sales team without management involvement are vanishingly small.

Let me repeat that point because it's often overlooked. Without a coach who can operate outside of the Drama Triangle—not just understand it, mind you, but consistently choose not to play any one of its roles during the coaching process—the odds for sustainable success are minuscule. Without both an organizational and personal commitment to the development of the salesperson, failure is not a meaningful learning experience. In that case, after failing at something, the salesperson moves through the familiar stages of denial, fear, anger, acceptance, and into the state of despair—and stays there. Without a coach who knows how to stay out of the Drama Triangle, the vast majority of salespeople never make the personal choice that something different has to happen and that they are the ones responsible for making it happen. Without a good coach, you don't get a salesperson who makes a decision and resolves (as a matter of personal integrity): "You know what? I'm never going to do that again. I have to find something new to do instead, and I have to get good at it."

To be sure, the management role I am describing and the model under which management receives training first (rather than the members of the sales team, who are typically perceived as being "the problem") is not the way most companies operate. Defending the distinction I have drawn your attention to in this part of the book is still very much a minority position in the business world. But that doesn't make it any less relevant, important, or, in the vast majority of Sandler client relationships, mandatory. Let's face it. On this particular issue—the issue of learning and how best to support it—the majority happens to be dead wrong.

In Part 4 of the book, we'll look closely at the three elements of the organization that must work together to establish, support, and deliver on the promises of a learning-based culture.

> *"Does history record any case in which
> the majority was right?"*
>
> —ROBERT HEINLEIN

PART 4

Accountability

CHAPTER 20

The Three Accountabilities

There are a lot of important differences between organizations that have a strong learning culture and those that don't. I've already shared some of those differences with you in earlier chapters. In this section, I want to share another critical distinction that will help you accelerate movement toward a culture of learning in your organization: the idea of accountability. Here as elsewhere, I'll be sharing my experience as someone who trains sales managers and sales teams and who has seen other parts of the organization adopt the same principles of accountability in order to support and sustain an organization-wide embrace of the process I call "winning from failing."

Organizations with a strong learning culture inevitably have a strong parallel culture of accountability. They are two sides of the same coin. Everyone involved in training and development initiatives operates at the level of personal commitment. In fact, at organizations we work with that operate at the high end of the learning-culture spectrum, there is a system for assigning clearly defined levels of responsibility to any learning initiative and, indeed, any initiative worthy of the organization's time, attention, money, or other resources. I'm talking about the well-known RACI system. Perhaps you've heard about it. If so, the points below will serve as a refresher. If not, it will serve as an essential introduction.

THE RACI SYSTEM

In any project, each team member is assigned one and only one of the following roles.

- **R = Responsible.** These are the people who do the actual work necessary to get the job done.
- **A = Accountable.** This is the one person who is ultimately accountable for the verifiable, measurable completion of the task and who delegates to those responsible.

- **C = Consulted.** These are the people whose counsel is sought and with whom communication flows in both directions during an initiative.
- **I = Informed.** These people are simply kept in the loop on the initiative's progress. Typically, communication with them is only in one direction, but they're free to weigh in at any time.

THE OPPOSITE OF RACI

By contrast, in organizations without a strong learning culture, people tend not to be accountable and responsible for much of anything. They operate under the principle that training is something for other people. No one person is accountable for the success or failure of any initiative so no one bothers to learn how to be.

Responsibilities and accountabilities in these organizations are loosely defined or not defined at all. Top management approves a training and development initiative, but sets no clear goals for it and does not measure its outcomes (beyond passing out "smiley-sheets" that ask people how much they enjoyed the experience). The training department is only responsible for delivering the training—disseminating knowledge. Participants are only responsible for showing up to the training event—and staying awake. That's it.

Most of the organizations we work with need our help because they do not have a strong learning culture in place. They haven't put a cultural premium on responsibility and account-ability, and this is a root cause of their productivity issues. They have never adopted the RACI system or anything like it. That means they have some work to do.

That's the reality, and I don't want to sugarcoat it. A culture of accountability doesn't happen overnight. It takes work and sustained effort over time to make a cultural change of that magnitude happen.

THE THREE COMMITMENTS OF FACILITATED LEARNING

So how do you get there? What are the components necessary for this kind of cultural change to happen? What has to be in place to make it work?

As it turns out, there are three pieces to this particular puzzle.

First and foremost, as mentioned earlier, you need a clear management commitment to a culture of learning. By "manage-ment commitment," I mean adoption of the RACI system by the person to whom the salespeople report and also by top manage-ment within the organization.

Second, you need a parallel training commitment that is oriented consistently toward a culture of learning. The training organization you choose must be professionally competent and objective. Often, it is best to have an outside entity coordinate with any internal training department initiatives.

Third, you need a commitment from the learners, also known as the participants, such that they are consistently, personally oriented toward a culture of ongoing learning and development.

FACILITATED LEARNING

Management Commitment   Training Commitment

Learners' Commitment

I've compared these three elements to a three-legged stool. If any one of the legs is missing, the stool tips over. If you have management on board with the accountabilities that support a learning culture and if you have training that is geared toward learning but you don't have salespeople who are willing, able, motivated, and committed to grow and learn, nothing is going to happen. You need all three accountabilities. (To continue the metaphor, you need something for the stool to stand on. That's the quality of leadership. You'll be learning more about that in the next chapter.)

In short: Management is accountable, the training organization is accountable, and the participant is accountable.* In the

---

* For an in-depth discussion of the coaching component of management's accountability, see Bill Bartlett's fine book, *The Sales Coach's Playbook: Breaking the Performance Code.*

chapters that follow, we're going to be looking at each of these accountabilities in depth.

Remember: To keep standing,
your three-legged stool needs all three legs.

CHAPTER 21

The First Commitment —Management

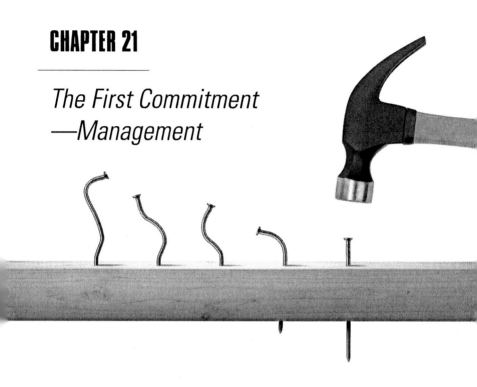

"Education is the kindling of a flame, not the filling of a vessel."

—SOCRATES

The first leg of the three-legged facilitated learning stool is management's commitment.

To what, exactly, is management committing? The three-legged stool of facilitated learning includes the process of going from knowledge to application to behavioral change. What you're doing as a facilitator of that is pretty simple: You're facilitating the learning to move forward, through action, into certain behavioral changes. You're not stopping at the dissemination stage. You're supporting people as they move forward to actual performance improvement. You're facilitating the process of turning knowledge into results. You're facilitating implementation.

Certainly, a good trainer has facilitator qualities. But it is not the trainer's formal responsibility to get salespeople into a state of improved performance. That's the manager's primary responsibility. If the manager for some reason can't personally be the kind of facilitator we're talking about, he needs to find someone who can be and delegate the task. He can never delegate the responsibility for implementing what has been learned. This is not the manager's only responsibility, of course, but it is a primary responsibility.

As we have seen, a manager has to have coaching skills, mentoring skills, supervisory skills, and training skills. What I want you to notice, though, is that all of these skills support the facilitation of the team's forward motion toward behavioral change and improved performance.

Let me say it again: Implementation of what has been trained is the sole responsibility of not the salespeople, but of management. Learning doesn't get implemented unless it has a facilitator. Someone has to be there to see that the training is implemented. Once the employees leave the training room, facilitation has to take place. Management is responsible for making sure that it does.

WHY THE FIRST COMMITMENT IS USUALLY ABSENT

To understand this, remember that there are two types of management: senior management (also known as staff management) and field management (also known as line management).

Senior management is responsible for the sales managers who work with salespeople in the field. Field managers report to senior managers.

Let's talk first about what typically happens with field management to undermine the first commitment. Typically, field managers select training that they liked years ago and that they assume everyone will benefit from and should take. Unfortunately, this is often not the case. The content may not be relevant or useful in any way to the members of the sales team who currently report to the field manager. However, that fact never makes it onto the field manager's radar screen. Years ago, the training was relevant to him. Years ago, it helped him. He assumes it will fix everything.

So the team is forced to take the training the field manager likes. After it's delivered, the field manager says things like, "You liked it, right?" Or, "It was great, right?" Everyone nods.

This is at its best "hopium" training (you hope it works) and at its worst "snake oil" training (you know it won't work, but you figure it can't hurt). When they're out of the field manager's earshot, standing around the water cooler, do you know what the team members say to each other? They say, "This, too shall pass." Most of the time, they're right.

This scenario seldom includes any meaningful attempt to measure the outcomes of the training. The HR people pass out smiley-sheets to find out whether or not people were "entertrained" by the session. If 50 people sit through it and no one complains (much), the field manager and HR assume the training was a success. But no one can point to any one behavior that has changed on the sales team, and no one can identify any metric that has improved as a result of that changed behavior.

How about senior management? How does the commitment fall short at that level?

At the end of the budget year, senior management wants to know the answer to one simple question about training and development initiatives: "What did we get for what we spent?"

When senior management poses that question, both the field manager and HR have a habit of going into "justify or defend" mode. HR sets out to prove that the organization got what it paid for: "They said they liked it." The field manager scrambles to justify the cost by trying to find some number—any number— that has gotten better since the training. (But notice that the number can't be tied to any specific behavioral change because no one has bothered to measure that.) If he can find a number that has improved, he says that measurement justifies the decision he made to go with X training. If he can't, he defends himself and says some variation of, "The trainer was bad." Senior management usually doesn't get the clear, unassailable ROI it's looking for, but they still nod and agree.

So what has to change?

Senior management needs to accept the responsibility of identifying the SMART goals that the training and development initiative must support. (That is, goals that are specific, measurable, achievable, realistic, and time-bound.) Field management needs to accept the responsibility to implement a learning and development initiative that supports those goals.

MOVING BEYOND "DID YOU ENJOY THE TRAINING?"

Committed, learning-focused leadership requires both kinds of management to challenge the organization to move beyond its institutional comfort zone. That means setting clear goals for the development campaign that connect to specific strategic objectives, and it means moving beyond questions like, "Did you enjoy the training?," to measure the campaign's effectiveness.

Many companies do not begin with this kind of commitment. There is no responsibility to identify a clear training goal that matches up with corporate goals. There is no responsibility to measure the degree to which specific competencies are mastered. Nor is there any responsibility to implement anything once the salesperson steps out of the training room. It's all very disconnected—and therefore very costly.

If there is committed, learning-focused leadership, there is ideally a clear strategic plan toward a specific developmental goal with fingerprints from the very top levels of the organization. Let's say there's a goal to enter a new market that requires the selling team to move from the status quo of a short sales cycle with an emphasis on fulfillment into a brave new world that features a long sales cycle and an emphasis on the collaborative development of a solution.

Guess what? The organization's training and development strategy ought to connect directly to the strategic goal of helping the salespeople make that (major) transition. Not only that, senior management needs to help create that plan, ensure that it's implemented, and measure its outcomes over time.

The training and development methodology, curriculum, and content for the team must connect to, and be measured against, clear strategic goals and the competencies that support those goals. Setting these goals and assuring that the behavioral changes associated with them are implemented is management's responsibility.

Begin with the end in mind.
Define success.
Work as a team.

CHAPTER 22

The Second Commitment —Training

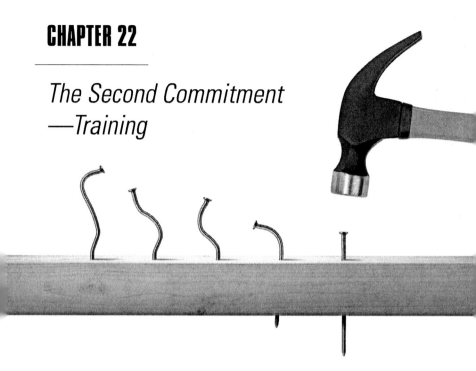

T he second leg of the three-legged facilitated learning stool is the commitment of a professional trainer.

On the surface, the criteria for fulfilling this commitment look pretty straightforward. The training the organization offers must be the appropriate content, structured within an appropriate curriculum; it must be relevant to the salesperson's world; it must be modeled consistently, in both words and actions, by management; and it must be delivered by a competent facilitator. (You remember our discussion of the facilitator's responsibility from the previous chapter.)

Fulfilling this commitment for the organization's salespeople should be a straightforward matter, but the sad truth is that very often it isn't. Typically, the big challenge lies in that final requirement, finding a competent facilitator—the professional trainer.

Very often, senior management believes that it has arranged for competent people to engage in the business of training salespeople. Instead, what has happened is that senior management has arranged for someone to tell salespeople things about selling. That's very different!

THREE RUNGS ON THE LADDER

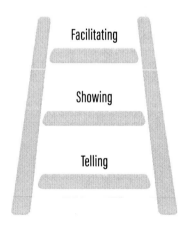

Telling means disseminating information. It means delivering instructional content. The person who is telling about the content may well have great communication skills, may well be personable, and may have a wonderful instruction manual to work from—and all of those are wonderful things. But none of what this person does should be mistaken for training because someone who is only telling salespeople what to do is not yet showing them how to do it.

Showing means demonstrating. Someone who is demonstrating a certain skill actually has the skills to do what is required, not just the theoretical knowledge. Ideally, there is the same ability as the telling option above to deliver the content along with good instructional content. What else is needed? That the person has the essential element of experience. Such a person not only tells salespeople about the content but also demonstrates the content to them on a personal level from a position of high integrity and credibility. This is not the same as simply teaching the content, which is actually telling the content. Most organizations fail their teams because they do not connect them with professional trainers who can actually do what they're teaching.

Line managers must be able to model the behavior in question. Otherwise, they are defaulting on one of their four big job duties (mentoring), and they can't possibly support and reinforce the training that's delivered. As a practical matter, this means that the line managers themselves must have taken, internalized, and personally implemented the same training the salespeople are taking. This is quite rare, and that's a problem. The trainer must be someone who knows how to "ride the bike." It must be someone who has ridden it many times, who has ridden it quite recently, and who knows, on a personal level, exactly what it feels like to fall while learning to ride. It's management's job to find and support such a person when it comes to securing the right one to set up and execute a sales training program. If management fails in that obligation, if it chooses instead someone who has never ridden a bicycle but has only read about it in a manual, then the second commitment will remain unfulfilled.

Facilitating is the next step on the ladder—the rung above showing. Ascending to this level means making sure the person executes the behavior in question in real time and is supported in doing so. Notice that I'm not saying the sales team's line managers must be the primary people who facilitate this learning in this way. It's perfectly OK for them to arrange for someone else to do it. I am saying, though, that they have to make sure the facilitation happens. The "do" rung of the ladder is the level of facilitation. It's what happens when someone engages one or more salespeople in real time as a result of debriefing with them about what just happened on a sales call and in so doing awakens that which has been trained. This is not easy. It's an advanced coaching function, and it's one of the things that a skilled outside trainer may be called in to do.

A poor instructor tells. A better instructor shows. A master instructor facilitates.

WHAT USUALLY HAPPENS

What usually happens when it comes to internal "training" initiatives for salespeople? (Note the quote marks.) Someone inside the company gets handed a training manual and is told, in so many words, "Hey, Overworked Eddie. Read this. Then train it next week."

Eddie dutifully lugs the manual home and stays up late "learning" it. He learns this content only for the purpose of regurgitating it—a process he calls, in all innocence, "delivering the training." As we've seen, though, that's not what it is. It may be the dissemination of information. It may be a revised take on product training, supplemented with all possible good intentions. It may even be a form of performance art. It may be any number of other things, including the traditional way that salespeople get trained. But when it comes to helping salespeople grow, it isn't professional training.

It's telling. It's someone in a room talking earnestly, but unpersuasively, about how to do something he hasn't done.

Remember—this is not Eddie's fault. He was told to do this. Therein lies the problem. People like Eddie are compelled to train content based on the information that's laid out for them in an instruction manual rather than from their real-world experience as sellers. Most of them are not sellers. Some once were, but that was a long time ago. Some are people who tried to sell and decided they couldn't. In many disciplines, including the discipline of sales, this is a recipe for a breakdown.

If training is to go beyond the level of telling, if it is to have any chance of actually supporting salespeople in the essential work of changing unproductive behaviors and replacing them with productive ones, if training is to rise to the level of competent professionalism, then the person who's doing the training must be able to climb all three rungs of the ladder.

LEARNING IS NOT AN EVENT

Before we leave this chapter, let me share a particularly critical point with you, one that most teams, unfortunately, don't address when designing training initiatives: Learning is not an event.

Training can be an event. Learning can't.

Learning is something that goes on as long as the person works for the company, in a way that is unique to the individual.

Let's look at both halves of that. First, learning has to be seen as continuous. Most organizations schedule a training event, or a series of them, and fail to schedule a developmental path of learning from that training. That's a huge problem. Seminars and training sessions can be great, provided that they fit into a development strategy and learning happens as a result of facilitated implementation of those events in the days, weeks, and months to follow. Too often, it doesn't.

Second, the learning that takes place has to be keyed to the specific challenges, aspirations, and growth opportunities of the individual employee. Not only does the learning need to take place over time, but it also has to be targeted to the learner in a way that makes sense strategically for both the organization and the person. Usually, this is not what happens. Usually, there is no diagnosis of individual performers and no learning path identified for that specific person. Management throws 30 or 40 people into a room, throws some training at them for a day or two, and assumes that what helped the line manager 15 years ago will be equally relevant to the people who are now forced to sit through the training. It's as though a doctor took 30 patients at a time, brought them all into a huge operating room, and said, "Right—nice to meet you all. I'm told you all have appendicitis. Let's start surgery."

This question of "diagnosis" of the individual salesperson, of the importance of establishing an individualized learning curve, leads to the third commitment: that of the learner, which I'll address in the next chapter.

> *"Tell me, and I forget; teach me, and I may*
> *remember; involve me, and I learn."*
> **—ATTRIBUTED TO BENJAMIN FRANKLIN**

CHAPTER 23

The Third Commitment —Learning

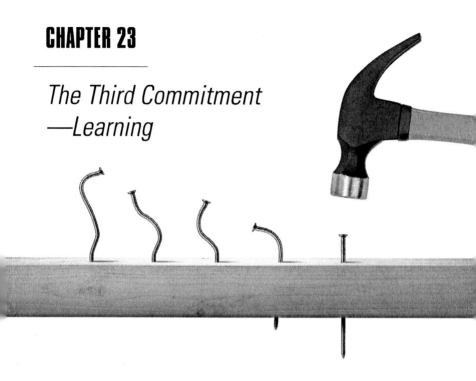

The third leg of the three-legged facilitated learning stool is the commitment of the learner.

The learner is the raw material. You can have very effective processes and all the support an organization can offer, but if you don't have the right raw material to introduce to the learning process, learning is never going to happen. You need a committed learner.

A committed learner is not the result of simply assigning people the responsibility to learn. All too often, salespeople are not committed to learning. Why is that?

There are a couple of reasons why people don't perform to expectations when it comes to learning.

1. They are unwilling (they won't learn).
2. They are incapable (they can't learn).

In other words, the learner has to be both willing and able. Let's look at the first criterion—being willing.

If salespeople are incapable of learning, it's a pretty safe bet you don't want them selling for your organization. If salespeople are not willing to learn, you're looking at essentially the same situation. It doesn't make any difference how able they are, how supportive they are, how competent they are, or how skilled they are. Learning is not going to happen. If they're not willing to learn and grow and they're still out there trying to sell for you, then all that has happened is that you have wasted a lot of money in terms of onboarding processes, support, training, and everything else.

Next question: How do you recognize a salesperson who is willing to learn? There are three clues.

First and foremost, this person has a powerful ambition, drive, desire, and passion for success. Note that this kind of passion is separate from a passion for learning. It's a passion for personal achievement. If your people have lost that passion for achievement or never had it, then you don't have the right raw material. That's just a fact. You've got low-octane fuel. It won't burn well. You might get something out of it, but you won't get the speed you're after. You can do all the training and conduct all the team-building events that you want. At the end the day, people will only learn to the level that matches their desire to achieve. If that desire to achieve is low or nonexistent, as is often the case, then learning will be low or nonexistent. The performance will be as well. That's reality.

Second, the learners must be driven to learn. That means they must have a no-matter-what commitment to learn as part of personal achievement—not a conditional commitment, not a "provided that" or "as long as" commitment—and they must be the ones who personally link achievement to learning. If you have a conditionally committed person, you have a conditionally committed learner. Again, you will be using low octane fuel.

The third essential element for committed learners is their attitude or outlook. This translates to self-worth. Those who have a deficit in self-worth (and there are plenty of them out there) inevitably find there is a parallel deficit in achievement. Their willingness to learn is compromised, as is their performance and (last but certainly not least) their overall quality of life.

There you have it—the three characteristics of a person who is willing to learn. If one of those three elements is missing, then by definition, you're looking at someone who is unwilling to learn. It's sad but true. Many, many people fall into the category of "unwilling but highly skilled."

In that situation, you have a choice. You can invest the time, attention, and resources to fix the problem (which is difficult and, in many cases, impossible), or you can let the person go or reposition him into another part of a company where these commitment deficits will not be such a problem.

I have to be very clear here—it is nearly impossible to turn such a person around. Often, managers get addicted to "hopium," perhaps because they don't want to face up to the emotional experience of letting an employee go. We often have to tell such managers, "You're not going to change that person—the tail on that dragon is just too long. Move them into another role. This individual shouldn't be in sales." (By the way, most training companies won't say this out loud because they don't want to lose out on training fees. But we at Sandler know that training someone who isn't committed to learning is a waste of everyone's time and energy, including ours.)

Think of your sales force as being made up of three groups with regard to production: the top 20%, the middle 60%, and the bottom 20%. You should be thinking of specific people who fall into each of these three groups. Got it? Great.

Picture your top-20% performers. What is your learning and development plan for those people? Most managers we talk to answer with some variation on, "If it ain't broke, don't fix it." Translation: Management pretty much gives them what they want (within reason) and leaves them alone.

How about the ones in your bottom-20% group? (Guess what? This is where the people who are skilled but unwilling to learn tend to live.) What's your plan for those individuals? Most managers we talk to tell a story of how they've gone into "close-correction supervision" mode with one or more of these folks. You know what that is: a long-term cover-your-anatomy project for HR so you don't have to deal with the hassle and emotional challenge of firing or reassigning someone. Basically, you're trying to harass these folks into leaving of their own accord, with lots of resources invested in the effort. It's a long-term strategy based on ignoring a performance problem. Ring any bells? I thought so.

How about someone from that third group—the 60% in the middle? What's your plan for that person? If you're like a lot of managers we talk to, you're at least tempted to share some of the training you received back when you were selling. One or two days taking the same medicine you took should help that person to get sharp and stay sharp, right? In fact, you may think, that "training" event would probably be perfect for everyone in the middle 60% group. Admit it—that kind of thought has crossed your mind, at least once. (Not unusual, by the way.)

I thought so.

Now let's examine a new possibility. Let's pretend you are looking for a 5% bump in income generation from the sales department as a result of your training and development plan this quarter. Let me suggest a scenario for your consideration.

Let's suppose you cut the bottom 20% from your team. You either fire them first thing tomorrow morning or reassign them to other roles in the organization. (That's up to you—all I want to propose is that you stop expecting them to sell for you, starting right now.) You redirect the savings and put it all into training resources for the top 20% of your team, meaning you run assessments, diagnose each individual, and set up a strategic development and coaching plan for each one of your most committed sales leaders. You leave the 60% alone.

If you were to do this, then I would be willing to make a prediction. I predict you will not only meet but dramatically exceed your 5% goal. In fact, the best research out there suggests that the increases you will see from the top 20% will be in the neighborhood of 100% in overall productivity for each salesperson.

Worth a try? I think so. What's standing in the way? Fear or force of habit.

Again—what do managers usually do? They do no assessment. They put the top 20%, the middle 60%, and the bottom 20% into the same training room. They assume that every one of those "patients" will benefit from the same medicine because it worked for themselves (or someone else) a few months, years, or decades ago. They do that even though they know for a fact that the ROI on the bottom 20% is going to be negative. How much sense does that make?

Once you've run the assessments with your people and

confirmed that the bottom 20% are uncommitted learners, we would advise you to not put them into the training room at all. To do so would be professional malpractice. Since they're not going to learn anyway, if you did take them into the training room what would they be? Hostages!

Also, if you assume that the same medicine will work for every patient in the room, then the vacationers—typically the 20% at the top—will be sitting there thinking about fantasy football when you're not looking (or maybe when you are).

You don't want hostages or vacationers in the training room or coaching sessions. You want committed learners.

To do that, you need accurate assessments of each salesperson. That means you need to know a lot about the person's professional competency strengths and weaknesses. Professional assessments are designed to give managers valuable information about a person's style as well as the behaviors and core competencies within the sales role. This battery of assessments identifies specific performance factors for the individual person (such as ambition and drive or the ability to qualify and close an account) so you know what is going on, right now, in this person's world. I guarantee you that the same thing is not going on in everyone's world.

Understand, please, that these assessments do not measure skills. They give managers a clear picture of the competency present (or absent!) within a specific person to perform in specific areas of vital importance to the person's role. If a competency is missing and you have "trained" the person to do something during a role-play that he can't do when in front of a prospect, you may wind up with a highly skilled salesperson who can't execute on that skill in real time.

Unless you can equip salespeople to perform under pressure, it doesn't matter how well they demonstrate something in a role-play. The learner commitment isn't there. You're fooling yourself.

Sometimes managers are surprised when we draw a line in the sand on the topic of learning commitment. But no one wants uncommitted learners in the training room. We're out to help companies achieve a clearly identified (and typically aggressive) financial goal. Since we have that shared objective with the client, wouldn't it make sense to do the X-ray before we start surgery?

"Any fool can know. The point is to understand."

—ALBERT EINSTEIN

PART 5

ROI

CHAPTER 24

"Why Are We Doing This, Anyway?"

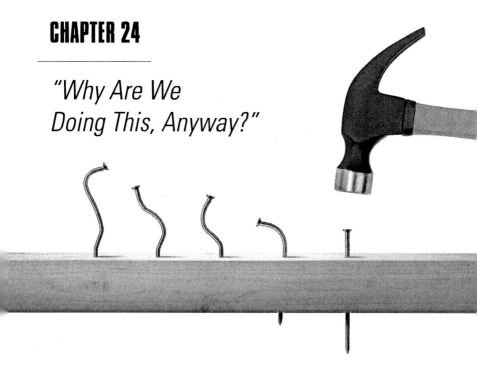

By this point in the book, I'm hoping that it's clear how often training and development initiatives can go wrong. Even with the best of intentions and the most impressive goals, even with a nice looking binder and a cool typeface, these initiatives can and do end up making a true learning culture more elusive than ever, and, all too often, undermining the organization's most important strategic objectives. Here are some examples of "failure precursors" that I believe you should now be able to spot easily. Do any of them ring a bell for some aspect of your organization or career?

1. The top salesperson becomes a manager and resolves to show the rest of the team "how it's done."

2. The new manager's "coaching" session, typically held in public, features some variation on the words, "Next time around, just do what I did back when I was selling, and..."

3. Management opts to deal with performance/quota challenges with one simple "big idea"—hiring a new round of "go-getters" who will quickly emerge as "role models" and "mentors" to the rest of the team.

4. Management assumes that each member of the team will benefit from the same training the manager received "back in the day."

5. Management and the training/HR team assume everyone on the team has the same skill deficit and arrange for a one-time "training" event designed to repair that deficit.

6. Someone who doesn't sell for a living, or hasn't sold for a living for a significant period of time, is selected to do the "training" that is supposed to help the sales team improve performance.

There are many more warnings signs of what I call "learning culture failure," but these will do for now. What I want you to notice is that each of the six undertakings I just shared with you violates a basic management rule, one I'm sure you've heard from multiple sources: Begin with the end in mind.

When it comes to developing a viable learning initiative for the sales team, you want to ask yourself a very simple question: "Why are we doing this, anyway?"

In other words: Why are you even trying to put together a program that will support the sales team? What's the point of doing that? Why should you bother training them in the first place?

Ninety-nine times out of a hundred, the answer is simple. You're doing it to improve your return on investment. Long before you have made any decisions about what the training and development strategy ought to be, you can start thinking about what you want to accomplish. At the end of the learning initiative, X months from now, what do you want to see change in a measurable way? Why will it have changed?

These are big questions. They demand thoughtful answers. To equip you to answer them, I need to introduce you to a learning measurement model that's specifically designed to deal with them. We'll look at that model in the next chapter.

"Begin with the end in mind."

—STEPHEN COVEY

CHAPTER 25

The Four Levels

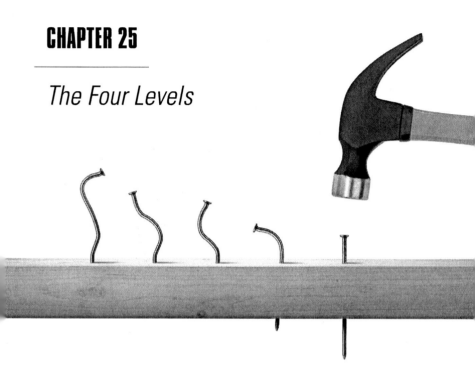

Back in 1959, Donald Kirkpatrick, a past president of the American Society for Training and Development (now ATD, the Association for Talent Development) first published what he called his Four-Level Training Evaluation Model. He updated the model slightly in 1975 and again in 1994, the same year he published his best-known work, *Evaluating Training Programs*. That model has been a standard in the world of training and development ever since, but a surprising percentage of corporate decision makers responsible for learning programs have never heard of it. That's a little bit like a NASA flight director never having heard of Isaac Newton. A few words of introduction to Kirkpatrick and his model are in order here.

Kirkpatrick's argument is that there are four measurements that always must be taken into account when approaching training. Once you determine what the development strategy is—in other words, what you're trying to accomplish, and what behaviors support that goal—you can establish the learning path and begin to measure effectiveness at those four levels. They are:

DONALD KIRKPATRICK'S FOUR LEVELS OF TRAINING

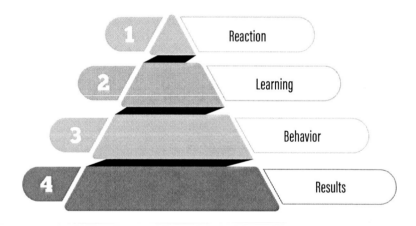

Most training organizations will measure to the first level, which is the level of reaction. They'll ask questions at the end of the training like: Did the trainees like it? What is the trainees' response? What was the reaction of the audience to the training? They'll pass out smiley-sheets. They'll do a survey. Of course, such assessments are highly subjective. If they do any analysis at all about return on investment, most organizations will only do it at this level.

The second level is learning. Here the questions are: What is the result of the training? What do the participants know now that they didn't know before, and what skills do they have now that they didn't have before the training?

This level is extremely important, yet most organizations don't consider it. You can measure for part of it with testing—the cognitive part. The skills piece, however, must be measured with demonstration and observation in a controlled environment, and there must be a measurable outcome. Notice that this level is still not focusing on behavior in a live selling situation, but only on what new skills have been acquired and can be demonstrated (in, for instance, a role-play.)

At the third level, the question is: As a result of the training, what behaviors changed on the job? This is a very different question, and it's a strategically important one because the behavioral change you're after must support the organization's strategic goals.

This is where you take your analysis to the field in the world of sales. Did any actual behavior change? If it didn't, the "training" was just another binder on the shelf. If you want to get a different result, you have to change the actual behaviors that take place on the ground. (Recall a well-known definition of insanity: doing the same thing over and over again, and expecting different results.) Very often, skills and knowledge don't change behavior.

Here's where reinforcement over time is important. Both for the salesperson and manager, there has to be access to coaching reinforcement in the likely event that things don't go perfectly the first time a salesperson tries to use the new skills or knowledge. If I'm that person, if I try something new and I don't have an ongoing support resource, it's highly unlikely I'm going to figure it out if I'm doing it right on my own. I'm going to revert to what I did before because at least that worked sometimes. The urge to survive is a much heavier emotion than the urge to try new things. Without ongoing reinforcement, the easiest path to survival will always win. People drop back to old behaviors.

This is a critical element when the salespeople go out into the field. Management must be prepared to provide reinforcement as they're executing the new behaviors they've learned. As we've discussed, that means setting up clearly defined areas within which it is OK for the person to fail and supporting the person such that execution of the new behavior continues even after failure. Remember: Give the learner permission to fail, but not permission to quit. If training is not reinforced in the field in this way, behaviors are not likely to change.

Worse, if the manager has been trained in a different skill, the behavior of the team can be expected to revert to a standard called "whatever the manager is most comfortable with." That means all of the training and development you've done becomes another binder on the shelf. Nothing more.

At level four, you look at results. The question is: What actually happened? This is a question decision makers are often very eager to pose, but they are likely to skip levels two and three when they pose it. This means they are unlikely to get meaningful information. (I'll talk more about this problem in the next chapter.)

At the fourth level, you determine if results are measured in a way that gives you any strategically relevant insights. Where are you? Are you getting closer to or further away from the goal you identified before you started the development initiative? That's a vitally important question, but you can only ask it after the initial reaction of the sales team has been assessed, after the learning has taken place and been measured objectively, and after the behavior has changed in the field and been measured objectively.

Those four steps of the learning model are essential to assessing the ROI of any training program. You can't skip any. If you do, you just have an outcome. You don't have any meaningful connections to anything that's gone before. Not only that—you need to measure all four simultaneously.

This point brings us to another big issue with this model. When managers first hear about it, they tend to think of the model as a series of checkboxes. You finish level one, move on to level two. You finish level two, move on to level three. Instead, it makes more sense to think of the model as a dashboard, one that you constantly consult, with four indicators.

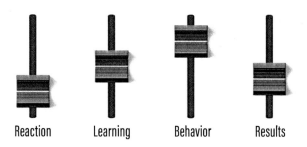

Reaction   Learning   Behavior   Results

This development cycle is a journey, not a destination. It is a process, not a one-time measurement. Your job is to measure all four indicators, all the time. If you don't—if you make the mistake of believing you can measure the first level once and then forget about it until the next big learning initiative—you miss the opportunity to see what the team's reaction is as the learning and reinforcement go forward. It's important to know the attitudinal response to what you're doing—not just once, but all the time. You need to know what impact your actions had on your team's reaction. You need to know what team members didn't know before, what skills they added, how they feel about implementing those skills, and how those attitudes affect behavior.

It's not uncommon that just one training session has a dramatic effect on performance in the field—but you need to know why that is. Are the team members excited about the prospect of earning more money by implementing the new skills? Or, are they changing behavior for the simple reason that they fear they're about to be disciplined? Those are two very different scenarios. You have to assess level one constantly. The same goes for levels two, three, and four.

This process is not a series of gates. It's a way of measuring and analyzing the team's performance on an ongoing basis.

In a learning culture, you constantly measure these four things. You're always going to get a result. The questions are: "Did we get the result we were after? Whatever the result, what caused it? And, why?"

The Kirkpatrick Four-Level Model is (embarrassingly) disregarded in many corporate learning environments. In the next chapter, we'll look at some of the consequences of that oversight.

"Never give up."

—SIR WINSTON CHURCHILL

CHAPTER 26

Meetings, Money, and Medals

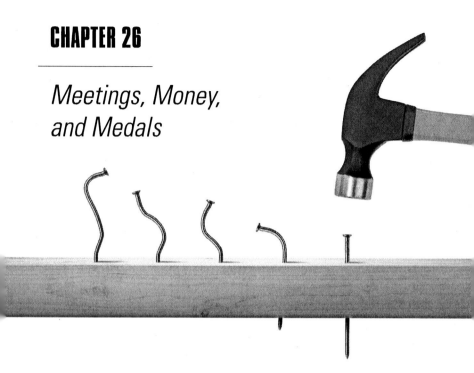

L et me preface what I have to say here with an important personal acknowledgment. When I say "management," I mean you and me. Everything I'm going to discuss management doing in this chapter, I've done myself. Please bear that in mind as you read.

In the real world, most of management's attempts to improve sales performance do not bother with any ongoing analysis of the four-level "dashboard" model I just shared with you. Most of the time, with the very best of intentions, leaders don't take on, in any meaningful way, the management job description elements of coaching, mentoring, and personalized training that I've been looking at so closely in this book.

Instead, what they usually do is one of three things that may feel familiar.

First, and most commonly, they focus on one-time motivational events that they can take part in with the team and then check off the list. These are usually meetings—something most people loathe—disguised as something else. The meetings could be one-day sales rallies designed to get the team "pumped up," they could be team-building initiatives, they could be some form of one-size-fits-all training, or they could be some other initiative that's meant to boost morale, raise spirits, improve cohesion, or whatever other buzzword is popular. Leaders may think they're motivating their team by taking them out to dinner. That kind of motivation may have some impact on the attitudinal picture, but, as a stand-alone event, it's unlikely to lead to sustainable behavioral change on the part of an individual salesperson. If leaders were honest with themselves, they would admit that.

Secondly, leaders utilize familiar incentives (meaning financial ones). An example would be a short-term contest promoting higher performance over a six-week period; the top 10% of performers win a financial or material reward of some kind. (They might win a vacation trip or be allowed to pick something out of a catalog.) Here's what you need to understand: Each and every person on the team is not going to be motivated by precisely the same thing. People are not always motivated by money and gifts. If you set up all manner of contests, bonus systems, and commission arrangements without engaging, on even the most superficial level, individual salespeople about what their most important goals are and why they are willing to commit to them, you won't get the results you're seeking.

Third, leaders focus on recognition. This recognition can take any number of forms, but it usually involves singling someone out as salesperson of the month, rookie of the year, comeback kid, most valuable player, or whatever new accolade is in fashion. It never ceases to amaze me how routinely management emphasizes recognition without making any attempt to determine whether being recognized is perceived as a positive or a negative by the recipient. Yes, many people crave the spotlight—but there are many other contributors on a team who aren't particularly eager to step into it. (This connects to the common problem of assuming that everyone on the team is a superstar in training, wants to be a superstar, or can become a superstar. I'll examine the impact of that dangerous myth in the next chapter.)

In the real world, leaders often fall back on meetings, money, and medals. In most organizations, that's the "way we've always done it." Sheer force of habit propels the backing of these initiatives, usually without anyone stopping to ask:

- "What is the impact of this initiative on our learning culture?"
- "Is any of this helping to improve performance in a measurable way?"
- "Is any of this supporting the professional growth of the sales team?"

All too often, if people are honest, they would find that the answers are: "Negative"; "No"; and "Not really."

Let me be clear. Meetings, money, and motivations are good tools. There's nothing inherently wrong with the choice to use them. They do work with some people. However, they don't work with everyone. Not only that, if they're the only tools that are being used, they can have a demotivating effect on most of the team. That may seem counterintuitive, but it's true. I'll explain why in the next chapter.

True motivation comes from within.

CHAPTER 27

The What and the Why

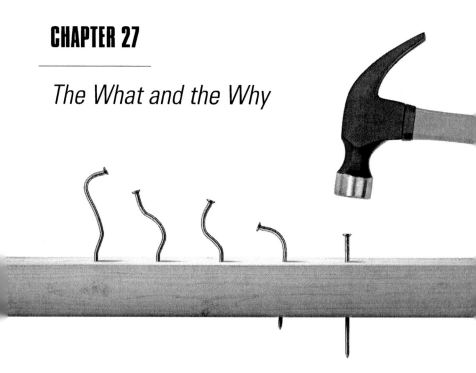

When it comes to learning and development initiatives, you need to know two things: the *what* and the *why*.

The *what* is strategic, ongoing development of the individual—as opposed to a single tactical training event or even a series of such events. That's the big takeaway from the chapter you just read. Don't fall into the trap of thinking you can fling the seeds out the window, drive away, come back in the fall, and find a crop that's ready to harvest. What we are talking about takes continuous effort.

The *how* comes from building and supporting learning. The focus is on developing the people, and the culture has to support that.

The *why* you're doing this is pretty simple. Ongoing support of individualized learning and development is the biggest and best investment you can make in your organization because it produces sales growth you can sustain. You're doing this because you want sustainable growth within the sales organization.

Let me make an important point, though. A learning culture doesn't cause sustainable growth to happen, just as the act of putting a seed in the ground, on its own, doesn't cause a crop to grow. There are a lot of factors in play: weather, soil, nutrients, birds that like to eat seeds—you name it. So you don't want to fixate too much on finding a single cause. You don't want to get into a debate about whether training is that cause. What you want to think about instead is supporting sustainable growth, and a learning culture does that. When you invest in the development of the people in your organization, you're seeding in the spring so that you can harvest in the fall. You can measure the yield of that crop. By the way, we'll be looking at how to do that—specifically, how to determine the return on investment for the dollars that get invested in development—in the next chapters.

Training and development won't ever be the sole cause of success, and similarly, they will not ever be the sole cause of failure. But they will contribute to both.

Let me throw another metaphor at you. Think of sustainable

growth in the sales force—the big *why*—as a building. Think of a learning culture as the mortar that holds all the bricks of that building in place. There are hundreds of bricks that will have a say in whether the building stands up or not: a leadership brick, a pricing brick, a product/service quality brick, a marketing brick, a customer-service brick, a commitment-to-innovation brick. All of those are going to have an impact on the structural stability of the building we call "sustainable sales growth." But at the end of the day, the only way those bricks are going to hold together, support each other, and do their job at maximum efficiency is if the people—the leaders, the managers, the salespeople—are strong enough to hold all those bricks together. By investing in the development of the people, you are helping them hold everything together. The mortar is only going to be as strong as you've developed the people to be. When the building is finished and occupied, you can't point to any individual brick and say, "That's why we've got a building." However, you can be sure that, without the mortar, the whole thing would be a pile of rocks.

Let's start by looking at ROI.

Stop simply spending money on training and begin investing in the development of your people.

CHAPTER 28

The ROI on Bricks and Mortar

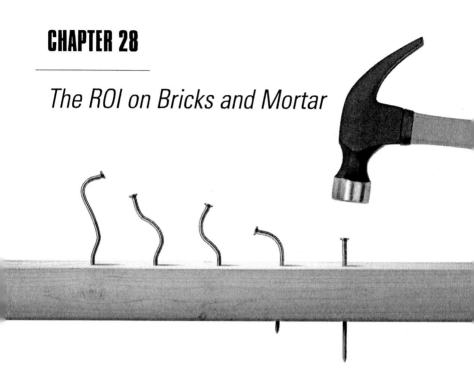

T he big question we at Sandler encounter, time and time again, is: "Is an investment in learning and development going to be worth it?" Or (more commonly) after the fact: "Was this worth what we paid for it?"

What can you know already, going into this? You know from our discussion of the Kirkpatrick model that you can't just measure the results of the sales team after the training is done. If you only measure results and nothing else, then all you have is an outcome. You don't have any valid cause-and-effect connection to what happened before. But if you incorporate the other steps we've discussed, you have a lot more information. You can identify the result, which maybe is good or bad, and see a correlative relationship with the training. You can confirm that the training you selected was appropriate to your strategic objectives. You can confirm how people reacted attitudinally to the learning initiative you put together. You can confirm that your people have now learned something and mastered a skill that they hadn't before. You can confirm that behaviors have changed as a result of people changing their patterns, and, finally, you can evaluate the outcome.

Let me emphasize once again that this is where reinforcement over time is important, both for the individual and the manager. There has to be access to coaching and reinforcement in the likely event that things don't go perfectly the first time a person tries to use the skill or the knowledge. Whether you're a salesperson or a manager, if you don't have a reinforcement resource, it's highly unlikely you're going to figure it out on your own. As we've seen, people without reinforcement are going to revert to whatever it was they did before. At least that worked sometimes, and they want to survive. They're going to choose the perceived route to survival—familiarity—over the actual route to survival—growth.

Once you've identified that X result took place, you have an outcome that can be logically connected to the change in behavior the learning initiative was designed to bring about. That's important. Now you are operating in the real world. From the reaction, you can prove team members went into learning; from learning, you can prove they went to behavioral change; and, as a result of that behavioral change, you can prove they delivered an outcome. But remember all four of those need to be measured all the time. To do that, as we've discussed, you first have to start with the end in mind. Just as you have to go from left to right when reading, similarly you have to start with the bigger objective before you start any learning and development initiative.

To get to a point where you can even evaluate the return on investment on your learning initiative—your campaign to strengthen that brick building—you have to start with the end in mind. You have to define what it is that you want out of this training and development strategy, which most organizations don't do.

So: What do you want?

It isn't, "I want better salespeople." That's not the result you're after. What is the result of getting better salespeople? More often than not, the people we talk to don't know. They come to us having self-diagnosed. "We need some training." "We want some team-building." "There's a morale problem." "Can you come by and do a day of training on prospecting?" They've already gone through this process in their minds before they reach out to us.

We at Sandler have found that, once we peel the onion back, once we ask: "What makes you think they need training in prospecting?" and continue with good dialogue, what clients come to us with at first is usually a symptom, not the problem itself.

That pain indicator tells us that there is some result that the organization wants but does not yet have. To deliver a program that can answer the question, "Was this worth it?," we have to sit down with the leader or company and make a better diagnosis. We do that by asking questions like:

- "If we were to change that thing that you say you want to change, what result would you experience?"
- "What larger goal are you looking to achieve as a result of doing this?"
- "What result would change if that would take place today, and how would you measure it?"

After a while, along comes an answer like this: "Well, we would have more in the pipeline, revenues would increase by 20%, and we would hit this quarter's target."

Great. Now is the time to figure out: What are the behaviors that would support that outcome, and why aren't they happening now?

Very often, people make the assumption that the cure for whatever they have self-diagnosed as affecting the team is training. There may be a problem with that. Training is a little like a drug. If you give a patient the right drug, of course, you can sometimes make the patient better. But if you give the patient the wrong drug, you can make the patient worse. You don't want to begin with the assumption that since you have the cure, you must have the matching problem.

Consider the situation of a software company targeting CPA firms in the United States as its customers. That company's leadership has decided that the team needs training in prospecting. Leadership says things like, "We need them on the phone more, and we need them to be better and more effective. So we've got to train hard on prospecting calls."

Now, let's say the team is trained hard on prospecting. Let's say the team then goes out and hits the phones, bound and determined to spend more time with and be more effective on prospecting calls. Team members do that from January through March.

Can you foresee any problem with a team of people striving mightily to get voice-to-voice prospecting conversations going with CPA firms in January, February, and March? I can.

That's tax return season. Even the accountants' clients can't get voice-to-voice contact during that period. In fact, the accountants' families probably can't either. The only things you're going to accomplish by ordering people to "be on the phone more" during the first quarter is to demoralize your team and damage your company's brand. You're going to be associated in the target customers' minds, not with great new software solutions that enable them to file returns more quickly and accurately, but with pushy salespeople who make life difficult for everyone in their office.

"Ready, fire, aim" will not work as a management strategy if you want to ensure that the learning initiative you set up gives return on investment.

The key to good training and development in a learning organization is to spend the necessary time up front to define the result you want. That's essential, not only in identifying the ROI of the learning initiative but to making sure it's the ROI you are seeking. More often than not, you will need some help from an outsider in defining the result and the best way to go about getting it. You will need a deep, thoughtful conversation to make sure you have the diagnosis and the treatment right. An outside perspective is usually essential to creating the right balance. Although you don't want to over-engineer your learning initiative, you also don't want to oversimplify it. If you've never done this balancing act successfully in the past, I would highly encourage you to reach out to a training professional.

Set your goals.
Define success.
Build your plan.
Engage your team.
Work your plan.

CHAPTER 29

Four New Questions

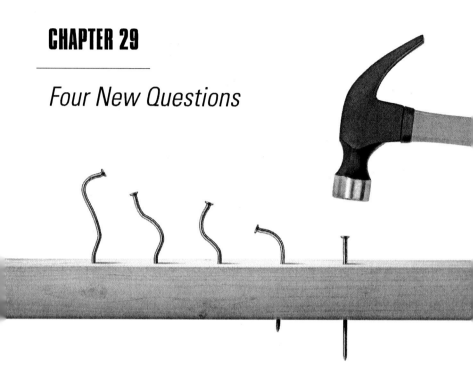

Based on everything we've examined up to this point, it's time to ask yourself a new set of questions. These questions can transform your learning initiative, your team's culture, and the culture of your organization itself.

The first one sounds like this:

"Based on a sound and careful diagnosis of our current situation, what behaviors, if any, would have to be adopted or be changed for us to get the result we want?"

Notice that vitally important phrase, "if any." This is not the time to make any assumptions. If new behaviors are not necessary, comprehensive training and development might not be the answer. It might be that you're doing all the right behaviors, but you're using them to penetrate the wrong market. You might have the right market, but the wrong product. You might have the right product, but you might be trying to sell it at the wrong time of year. And so on.

If you confirm something does need to be done differently, you can back into the next question, which sounds like this:

"Given that we want X behaviors to change, what knowledge and skills are necessary for our people to adopt and perfect those new behaviors?"

Once those are identified, you can ask yet another new question:

"What methodology will most effectively deliver that skill and that knowledge?"

Then, when you know what the right methodology is, you can ask the fourth critical new question:

"How should the learning be reinforced over time?"

These are not necessarily easy questions to answer. They take some time to pose properly and discuss (I've given you abbreviated versions as a starting point). They are likely to require thoughtful contributions from multiple parties before you can arrive at the best, most accurate answers. But there is a huge competitive advantage in investing the time and political capital necessary to answer these four questions. Once you make that investment, you have a comprehensive learning program. Every step of the way, everything you're doing can be measured. (By the way, you can always measure what you're doing. You don't have to wait until the training is conducted. You can measure what you're doing right now.)

THE FOUR QUESTIONS

1. "Based on a sound and careful diagnosis of our current situation, what behaviors, if any, would have to be adopted or be changed for us to get the result we want?"
2. "Given that we want X behaviors to change, what knowledge and skills are necessary for our people to adopt and perfect those new behaviors?"
3. "What methodology will most effectively deliver that skill and that knowledge?"
4. "How should the learning be reinforced over time?"

I need to emphasize once again that none of these four questions can be intelligently approached until you have established a clear strategic goal that makes sense for both the organization and the sales team.

There's an old saying that a journey of a thousand miles starts with a single step. That's true. But it's also true that a journey in the wrong direction starts with a whole bunch of steps that you end up having to retrace.

One you have identified the new result, once you know the behaviors that support it and the skills that support the behaviors, and once you know that the training and the reinforcement around all of that makes sense, that's when you can plan that first piece of training. You don't know where to begin until you reach that point.

Even when all of that is planned out, you still have preparations to make. Well before you launch any learning initiative, you want to step back and find out who knows what. This brings us to another critical topic: assessment.

Challenge your organization to ask the tough questions.

CHAPTER 30

Benchmarking

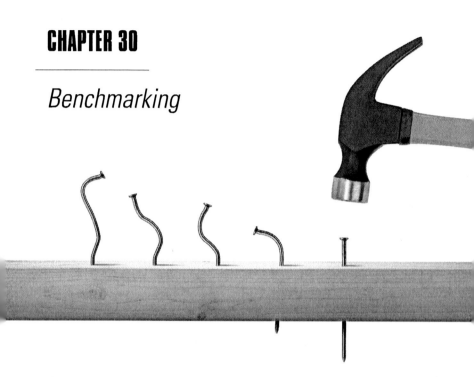

O nce you've answered the four big questions from the prior chapter—in detail, and ideally with the benefit of guidance from someone who's got both experience in the world of learning and development and the perspective of an outsider—once all of that is planned out and you know what you're doing, why you're doing it, and how to measure it, you want to step back and ask yourself exactly where each member of the team is, right now.

You have to find out where your people are in their personal development path. Why? Because you don't want to throw everyone into the same training room on the assumption that everyone has the same competencies as everyone else.

Here is the reality. Some people on your team are going to have skill sets that are far more refined than other people's and are going to be more comfortable leveraging those skills. Does it make sense to put those highly skilled people into the fundamentals class that might make perfect sense for newbies? If you happened to run a newspaper and you were lucky enough to have Ernest Hemingway on your team, would you make him sit through a freshman writing seminar that might make sense for your brand new hires? Of course not. His skill set would be so much higher than that.

It's the same with salespeople. Not only will forcing experienced performers to sit through "Selling 101" not give them anything new they can use, but it may also negatively affect their attitude when it comes to working for the company. (Of course, there are going to be situations where it makes sense for a veteran to take a refresher course on certain fundamentals, but even in those cases, the larger point remains: You have to do an assessment if you want to identify who these people are.)

Assuming that everyone on your team operates at the same level is a great way to degrade and even destroy the learning culture of the organization. In fact, if you were looking for an effective way to turn your best people against you, you've just found it. Make them sit through training from which they are convinced they will not derive any benefit. Make them part of the "hostages and vacationers" syndrome I've discussed elsewhere in this book.

Take the time to figure out where people are right now. Benchmark the individual members of your team before you launch the learning initiative.

Benchmarking includes identifying the kind of selling that supports the specific strategic goal driving the learning initiative. For instance, it might involve learning how to get C-level decision makers on the phone for a strong initial conversation that results in a scheduled second call or visit. Benchmark exactly what you want to see regarding the competency level for the skills you're developing. How many dials do you want to see from each team member per day? How many discussions? How many second meetings? Set a foundational level for where you want each person to be, and then find out exactly how close your people are to that target. Specifically, you will want to figure out:

1. **What they know, as well as what they don't.** Having an intellectual understanding of what goes into a good prospecting call with a C-level contact is important, but it's not the whole picture.

2. **What skills they have, as well as the skills they don't have.** Can the person deploy the skills necessary to conduct

such a call with a C-level prospect during, for instance, a role-play?

3. **What behaviors they're displaying when they're out in the real world, as well as what behaviors they aren't displaying.** How does that measure up with your targets? How many calls are being made? How many conversations with C-level decision makers are taking place? How many second discussions are being scheduled? How close are these to the foundation levels you've set?

Often, management assumes that the absence of a certain kind of behavior from a salesperson signals a skill-set problem. In fact, this may be a sign that the person simply isn't leveraging a skill that has already been learned. The big question is: Why?

This kind of intelligent, pragmatic, responsible pre-launch assessment of where your people are right now is essential. In addition to performance metrics, we at Sandler use tools like the Devine inventory and the wide range of assessments available from Extended DISC. Our experience is that working with these tools is a strategically sound first move for just about any learning initiative, but the design of the optimal assessment will vary by company. This is something you'd need to talk over with a professional.

Don't assume you already understand where each team member is in their personal development cycle. Find out for sure. Compare what you learn to the right benchmarks, and plan accordingly. Your goal should be to create differentiated instruction paths that serve all the different groups of learners on your team. That's a far better way to go than the one-size-fits-all approach most companies take. Most companies take someone who has five masters degrees and three PhDs and asks that person to sit all day with the high schoolers. That's not your ideal path. It's likely to be counterproductive, a waste of time and energy for everyone, and something that will end up lowering your return on investment and undermining your learning culture.

To support the strategic goal you've identified and achieve the ROI you want, set up an intelligent, targeted learning initiative that makes sense for the team as a whole and each member of the team. Make sure the program you launch makes sense for everyone on the team. You don't want to throw everyone into a training room, do some training, and hope that eventually some good stuff filters in. That's kind of like pouring gas all over the car and hoping it sinks in somewhere. It's not just counterproductive—it's dangerous.

If it is important, measure it.

CHAPTER 31

Connecting the Dots

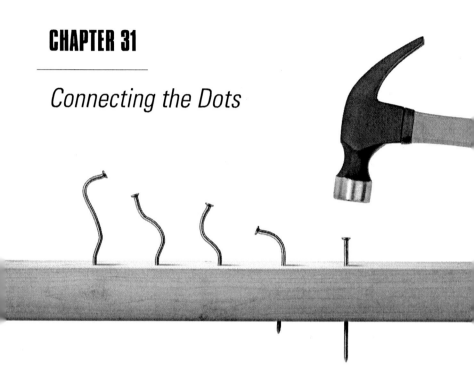

As we've discussed, measuring all the individuals in the group against the ideal that you want to see in the best-case scenario is benchmarking, which is followed by assessment.

Assessments let you know what the raw material is. Assessments tell you what team members know, how competent they are, and how skilled they are. The benchmark you establish in any given area is a target. It tells you where you want a specific salesperson to go as a result of the learning initiative.

Only when you know where people are and you compare that

to where they need to be can you design learning that makes sense regarding the organization's strategic goal.

It's essential that you do that kind of discovery because guesswork is just not enough. You may figure out that someone is a PhD in one area of selling, but is in elementary school in some other area. If you don't do an assessment, you end up going by your assumptions and gut instincts. All too often, assumptions and instincts are dead wrong. You need the real data.

Once you've done your job right, you can identify a specific area with a specific learner where the behavior has to change to support the organization's strategic goals. Sometimes you find that the behavior starts changing during the assessment phase simply because measurement has begun. Sometimes the fact that people know you're doing the assessment is enough to change the behavior. But usually, you need to go a little further to sustain a productive, strategically sound behavioral change over time.

I need to emphasize here once again that training and development can't fill all the gaps.

If you don't have the right product for the market, there's no amount of training that's going to change that situation for the better. If you create a new line of dog food but the dogs don't like it, you have to start with the dog food recipe first. There are always many elements to consider: the product or service; the market; the sales team; leadership decisions; distribution; the brand; and on and on. Sometimes people don't want to look at all of those issues critically. There may be an attitude that reverts to the common default positions: "If there's a problem with sales, that means we need training." Then: "The training is over and we still aren't getting sales—it must be the training's fault."

This attitude is so common that, sometimes, it seems that training and development are the outcasts of all corporate initiatives.

It doesn't have to be that way. When you look at your desired result first and work to build a learning initiative that supports that outcome, when you set the right benchmarks, when you look critically at the real-world behaviors and skills that support the role, when you assess the participants to figure out where they are before the training begins and where they are when the training is complete, when you create an individualized learning initiative that addresses all of the key elements, then you have created a complete learning and development initiative.

This kind of approach to learning tells you not only what kind of training strategy makes sense for the individuals, but also what kind of measurable progress they've made as you've implemented it. You know the training was appropriate. You know your team members have learned something or mastered a skill that they hadn't before. You know that behavior has changed as a result of that training. Out of all that, you know that X result took place that can be connected to the change in behavior.

When you measure progress all along the way, you connect all the dots. Then, you find that it's much easier to sustain incremental growth because you can say with confidence whether what you're doing is working. As a result, you know whether to do more or less of it. Now, you have real ROI measures for training and development. (And yes, all the principles I've shared with you here can be adapted to teams that do things other than sell.)

A motivation for moving from event-based training to a learning culture is realizing the value of moving from spending to investing.

CHAPTER 32

*Certified Learning and the
Culture of Success*

Y our goal, as I have mentioned, is to address the seemingly simple question, "Was the investment in training worth it?" As you've seen, you have to be prepared to measure activity and results if you expect to be able to answer that question. If you don't measure what's happening, you have a result but you don't know why you got it. On the other hand, if you are measuring development along the way, measuring the growth at all the relevant levels, then, when you get the result, you can directly point to where it came from, whether it's good or bad.

A learning initiative should cause a specific desired behavioral change, one that you can describe before the initiative even begins. If it does, you're going to get a meaningful result. If there's a problem, you can identify what the problem was. Was the skill not learned? Was it not implemented? Was it implemented, but were there other factors that affected the result? Measuring along the way tells you how close you're getting to the goal you've identified. This makes it much easier to cause incremental growth for each member of the sales team.

Before I leave you, let me share with you the critical point on which this book, and the entire Sandler training program, is based.

Continued learning through controlled
failure defines a learning culture.

There is a paradox at work here. Building a culture of success means building an environment where it is OK to fail—but not OK to quit or to stop learning and growing.

Effective leadership reinforcement, as we have seen, means identifying, ahead of time, the areas within which failure can occur, and then accepting that failure as part of the learning process when it does take place. If you don't give salespeople borders within which they can fail, then you have got a dysfunctional culture, not a learning culture. You have to have an environment that allows for controlled failure. People learn more, far more, from failing than they do from success. That's the human condition. To experience ongoing sustainable growth, you have to build learning and sustainable behavioral change into the culture. It's a big job.

I hope this book has helped you to reach a place where you and your organization can begin doing it.

Everyone needs continued learning.

EPILOGUE

The Opportunity

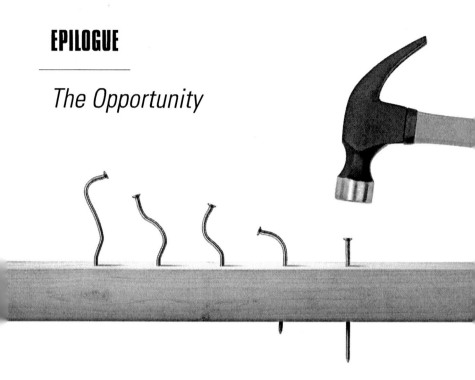

I f I've done my job and you've done yours, we've got an
opportunity.

Having made it this far from the beginning of the book,
you now know many great things about learning and development—what works, what doesn't, what a learning culture looks
like, and so on. But if all you've done is read this book—and thus
far, that's all I've asked you to do—there's a challenge to face,
one that I want to be sure you don't ignore.

You'll remember that Success Triangle I mentioned. Do you

recall its three sides? They are attitude, behavior, and technique. I'm hoping that, at this stage, given what we've gone through together, you now have a starting point for evaluating some new techniques when it comes to designing and implementing an effective learning initiative. You know a lot more about learning and development than you did before you picked up the book, but knowledge is not enough.

If your aim is to change a culture—you need to start on the personal level. That means moving beyond what you know. In addition to the right knowledge, you need to now apply it yourself and within your organization. You will then begin to acquire the skills needed to change the behavior of your organization— forming habits of learning and development activities that happen every day, from second nature. That typically involves working with a coach, and it's the whole reason Sandler is here.

You now have the opportunity to build a learning culture within your organization—but that kind of culture starts with one person. That one person, I suggest, is you. Please reach out to us so we can help you launch.

Visit us at www.Sandler.com and connect
with a Sandler trainer near you.

CERTIFIED LEARNING PATH

Sandler Training has developed a certified learning path that is built around the principles of this book. Using it, you can measure ROI. Sandler set four standards for learners who work with us: Bronze, Silver, Gold, and Master. (By the way, those four designations correspond to the four levels I shared with you earlier that you always want to measure.)

- A Bronze designation certifies that the person has learned the foundational knowledge necessary to begin the development process.
- A Silver designation certifies that the learner can demonstrate the skills necessary to perform the role effectively and that these skills make strategic sense to both the learner and the organization.
- A Gold designation certifies that the learner not only has the skills but has executed them as a part of an ongoing behavioral plan in the field, on the job.
- A Master designation certifies that the learner has achieved a set of challenging personal and professionals goals and results that support the organization strategically.

Sandler is the first training and development company to provide certified learning at all four of these levels for clients across the globe.

Remember the vital importance of the three-legged stool discussed in this book. Accountabilities within these three roles are what make Bronze, Gold, Silver, and Master certification possible. The three legs of the stool are:

- Instructor/content developer
- Learner/participant
- Management/leadership

All three of these players must do their job. If one of those breaks down, you can't expect to get the desired result. The degree of success is dependent upon the combined strength of the three legs. I can't emphasize too much the importance of keeping everyone accountable for delivering a return on that investment by measuring progress as you go. If the three groups don't work together to measure what's happening, the organization keeps throwing more money at the problem and nothing much changes—except, of course, the number of unread binders of forgotten training material sitting up on the shelves.

That's an extremely expensive approach—one you want to avoid. The key is measurement. Measured training and development hold everyone appropriately accountable for the role.

The trainer supports the learning, but cannot cause learning to happen. It's the participants who have to learn. To ensure that the trainer is doing the job, you must be able to measure that, too. Provided trainers are doing their job and salespeople learn what they're supposed to learn, implementation is the job of management. That responsibility cannot be delegated to the trainer or the learner. Once again, everyone must be held accountable.

For more information on certified learning, visit:
www.sandler.com/our-approach/sales-certification

Look for these other books
on shop.sandler.com:

Prospect the Sandler Way

Transforming Leaders the Sandler Way

Selling Professional Services the Sandler Way

Accountability the Sandler Way

Selling Technology the Sandler Way

LinkedIn the Sandler Way

Bootstrap Selling the Sandler Way

Customer Service the Sandler Way

Selling to Homeowners the Sandler Way

Succeed the Sandler Way

The Contrarian Salesperson

The Sales Coach's Playbook

Lead When You Dance

Change the Sandler Way

Motivational Management the Sandler Way

Call Center Success the Sandler Way

Patient Care the Sandler Way

CONGRATULATIONS!

Winning from Failing

includes a complimentary seminar!

Take this opportunity to personally experience the non-traditional sales training and reinforcement coaching that has been recognized internationally for decades.

Companies in the Fortune 1000 as well as thousands of small- to medium-sized businesses choose Sandler for sales, leadership, management, and a wealth of other skill-building programs. Now, it's your turn, and it's free!

You'll learn the latest practical, tactical, feet-in-the-street sales methods directly from your neighborhood Sandler trainers! They're knowledgeable, friendly, and informed about your local selling environment.

Here's how you redeem YOUR FREE SEMINAR invitation.

1. Go to www.Sandler.com and click on Find Training Location (top blue bar).
2. Select your location.
3. Review the list of all the Sandler trainers in your area.
4. Call your local Sandler trainer, mention *Winning from Failing* and reserve your place at the next seminar!